TIME TO THIN

TIME TO THINK

Mark Barnes

I would like to thank everyone who has contributed thoughts and ideas that have come to fruition in Time to Think. I would like to recognise the individual contributions of Julie Malik for word processing and layout, and Paul Richardson for his cartooning skills. Thanks also to Catie Barnes for inputting raw text and David Phillips for his technical knowledge of email – both making their debuts as part of the Step System Team!

This book is dedicated to Mary-Jane for making me 'want to bother'.
There are some great ideas in this book – let's keep working on them together!

First published in 2007 by Management Books 2000 Ltd
Forge House, Limes Road
Kemble, Cirencester
Gloucestershire, GL7 6AD, UK
Tel: 0044 (0) 1285 771441
Fax: 0044 (0) 1285 771055
Email: info@mb2000.com
Web: www.mb2000.com

Printed and bound in Great Britain by 4edge Ltd of Hockley, Essex – www.4edge.co.uk

British Library Cataloguing in Publication Data is available

ISBN 9781852525385

Contents

CHUCK!
NOT IMPORTANT!
OF NO USE
2000 REPORT
BLAH
BLAH
YAK YAK YAK

Contents

Key to symbols used throughout this book:

Question

Answer

Tip

Instruction

Case study

Introduction

- A matter of time
- How to get the most from this book
- Developing your skills
- Time Management Effectiveness Wheel
- Debriefing your Effectiveness Wheel
- The three boxes
- Action plan

A matter of time

Prior to the Industrial Revolution, ours was an agricultural society where ordinary people lived by the seasons and managed activity around the available daylight hours. Their motivation for activity was largely 'needs'-driven.

With the arrival of the factory system however, there was a need to establish clear working parameters, to have pre-determined work start and finish times and to operate transport and distribution systems to timetable. For the first time, people used diaries, or appointment books, and needed to be assured that different parts of the country were using a common time system. (Previously, for example, regional clocks had often been out of time with those in London – causing considerable confusion for travellers.)

The period of societal change from agrarian to industrial, threw up some interesting anomalies. One example is 'mill time', which was used in water-powered textile mills in the North of England.

Under this system the water wheel that powered the machinery in the mill would also drive the mill clock, which showed a ten-hour 'mill time' – the length of a 'normal' shift. The mill clock was set to keep pace with chronological time, *only when the water was flowing at a 'normal' pace.* If the flow slowed, it would cause the machinery running rate to slow and 'mill time' would also run slower, guaranteeing that every shift produced the same output – even though in real terms the length of the shift and the hours worked would vary.

This increased awareness of the link between 'time spent' and 'achieving the output required' (which in turn strengthened the link between time investment and monetary value) led to time being seen as a basic organisational measure and to the prevailing western views that:

- time is a resource.
- time is scarce.
- time is money.

Eventually, the need for a common understanding of 'time' also led to the development of international time zones – however, even within these there remain local anomalies, with many geographic areas and organisations within established time zones continuing to adopt their own time systems.

The perspective continues to change as demonstrated by the way in which 'normal office hours' in the UK (once, the 9-to-5 working day), have come under attack from a number of sources: from flexi-time; from the use of contractors or employees working away from home and so being happy to 'work later' than on-site employees; from Sunday trading, and so on. In continental Europe, we can see northern European companies imposing their early starts on southern European trading partners, who have historically taken a longer lunch break and continued to work later into the evening.

There is also an additional challenge for any individuals whose business demands that their networks of communications are global and who may find themselves 'getting in early to speak with Asia' and 'staying late to speak with the US'; working on Sundays with colleagues in the Middle East and losing the British 'Boxing Day' to all those countries of the world for whom it is an unknown concept.

At the same time, feeling obliged not to finish early (which in fact has come to mean feeling obliged not to finish on time, but instead to stay late), working from home, being based 'in the field' and having access to technologies that speed up pace and increase the ease of communication all add to a time related pressure.

Employers can no longer run 'mill time', but they do demand increased output in order to respond to competition or their customers' expectations. The unspoken truth is that an individual's time is less important than getting the job done and as a result, people put themselves under pressure to complete tasks and to 'clear the desk'.

With the heat turned up under the pressure cooker and with people feeling the need to deliver more, at a faster rate, they inevitably respond to the demands of the business by working harder, sacrificing their own personal time, dealing with immediate issues and only dealing with bigger and more complex tasks as the deadline for delivery becomes more proximate.

So, consider this. Have you ever run out of time on a project? If you have, where in the project did you feel the real pressure of running out of time? The chances are that it was at the end. The truth is that time is already slipping away for everything that we want to do. The problem is that we often do not realise it, until our failure to achieve is staring us in the face.

Many people who do not proactively plan to use their time well are amazed to find how quickly it slips away. They are so busy, that they do not have time to plan in the first place, and perhaps fool themselves into thinking that they are gaining an edge, getting things done by the skin of their teeth, because they 'work better under pressure'. This is a route to inefficiency and stress and there is an alternative...

Take responsibility because...

"...left to themselves, things tend to go from bad to worse"

The link between time management and personal organisation on the one hand, and life balance and stress management on the other, becomes increasingly clear.

To get to grips with this, individuals need a sense of perspective, to value 'self' and have a willingness to take responsibility for their own destiny. If people feel themselves to be valuable, then they will believe that their time is valuable, and as a result will want to use it well.

This desire will prompt them to become increasingly proactive in developing a disciplined approach to the management of time, tasks and people; to set themselves goals or objectives, and to plan and prioritise, finding ways to work smarter, rather than harder – all of which has the effect of leaving them feeling in control and rather better positioned to drive towards achieving their own definition of success.

Many people understand that the best way to achieve any certainty about their own future is to create and nurture it themselves.

But there is a dilemma. Whilst it is important to focus on the long term, should it be done at the expense of the proximate, the urgent, the short term?

Isn't it time to think and to ask:

"What am I doing about my short-term plans?", and to question in parallel:

"What am I doing in the short term to move my bigger plan forward?"

It might also be useful to come to terms with some simple truths:

- ❑ There is no formula which gives anyone a one-person-sized job.
- ❑ No-one can provide a 'time management injection' to help others to organise and utilise their time resource better.
- ❑ No-one can conjure up an extra few hours in a day for themselves or anyone else.

Whilst we cannot 'make time', we can spend it in such a way that we can optimise usage and provide the best possible return on our investment.

A small amount of time spent organising and planning can pay huge dividends, if it enables us to spend our scarce resource doing the right things, right first time.

How to get the most from this book

Our time, along with our health, is probably our most valuable asset. Time is also the most egalitarian of resources. We all have 24 hours in a day, 7 days in a week and 365 days in a year. So, why is it that some people are so much more productive than others? Invariably, the reason is that they have taken proactive decisions about what it is they want to achieve, as a result of which they are able to focus on doing the most appropriate things.

This book is intended to help you to reflect on your personal use of time, the way that you process tasks and how you can get the best from your interactions with others.

Each chapter is a mix of thought-provoking content, questions and exercises. You can either work through the book chapter-by-chapter or dip in and out as you would like.

Some chapters will demand an investment of time over a sustained period, but the effort involved will result in both high quality data and improved outputs.

This kind of focused self-management requires proactive planning, allied with appropriate tools. It demands positive action in taking control of one's own surroundings – the working environment and the myriad of potential interruptions and distractions that surround and sometimes seem to conspire against us.

This book will enable you to:

- ❑ review your current use of time and enhance your personal effectiveness in all aspects of work.
- ❑ review your implementation, task management and other existing organisational tools.
- ❑ feel in control, prioritise and plan to do the 'important'.

...and it will provide stimulation, ideas and the motivation necessary for you to move forward with positive change.

If nothing else, it will help you take some Time to Think!

People who are effective focus on key success criteria. Using the group headings Technical, Tactical, Fitness, Mental and Lifestyle, I have created a Time Management Effectiveness Wheel (see Figure 3) which captures twenty of these criteria, one per segment.

Developing your skills

Self-scoring – use the mechanism below to identify your strengths and areas for development. This in turn will highlight the areas of **Time to Think** that you would most benefit from reading and will enable you to create a personal action plan.

The wheel has a scoring mechanism, which runs from 0 at the centre (the lowest score), to 10 at the outer edge (the highest score). Your personal score will fall somewhere between these two extremes!

Step 1 – think of yourself in the workplace. How would you score yourself in each of the segments currently? (See Figure 1.)

Mark or shade your score with a highlighter pen, as shown in the diagram on the right. Do not be tempted to score ten out of ten for everything, but use the full range of scores.

Add up your total cumulative score from every segment and enter it into the current cumulative score box over the page. Then divide the figure by two, to convert the score into a percentage. Enter this new score into Box A, as shown.

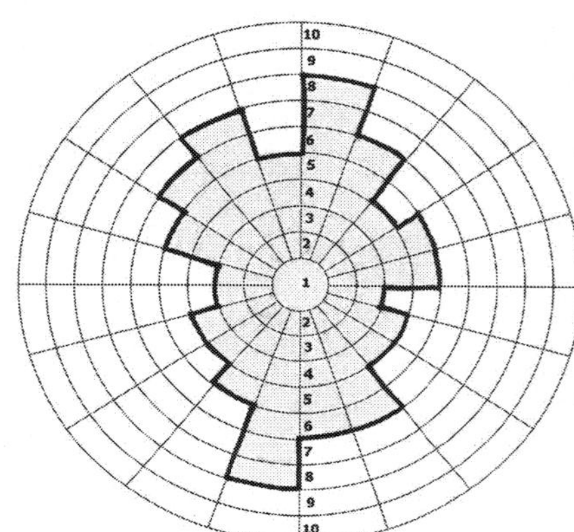

Figure 1

Step 2 – now revisit the Effectiveness Wheel and with a different coloured highlighter pen, identify those areas where you think either you could, or should, move the score forward, (see Figure 2).

Again, be realistic. Do not assume that you can move all of the scores forward to be ten out of ten. Look instead for real areas of opportunity to raise your game.

Once completed, add up the new total shaded area, divide by two as previously and put this new score into Box B.

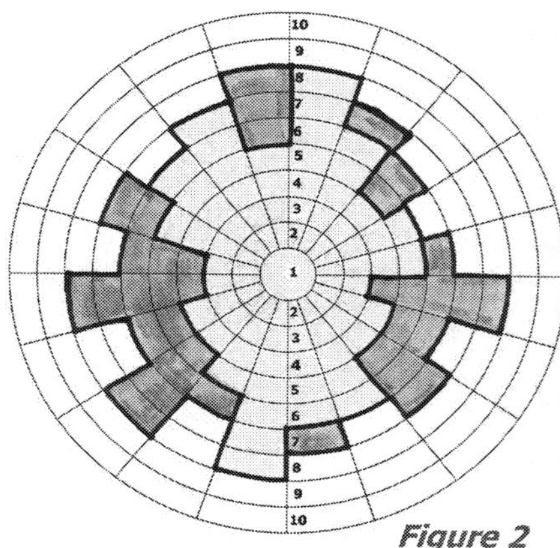

Figure 2

Step 3 – find the difference between Box A and Box B. This represents 'the % Gap' – your opportunity to develop and to raise your game.

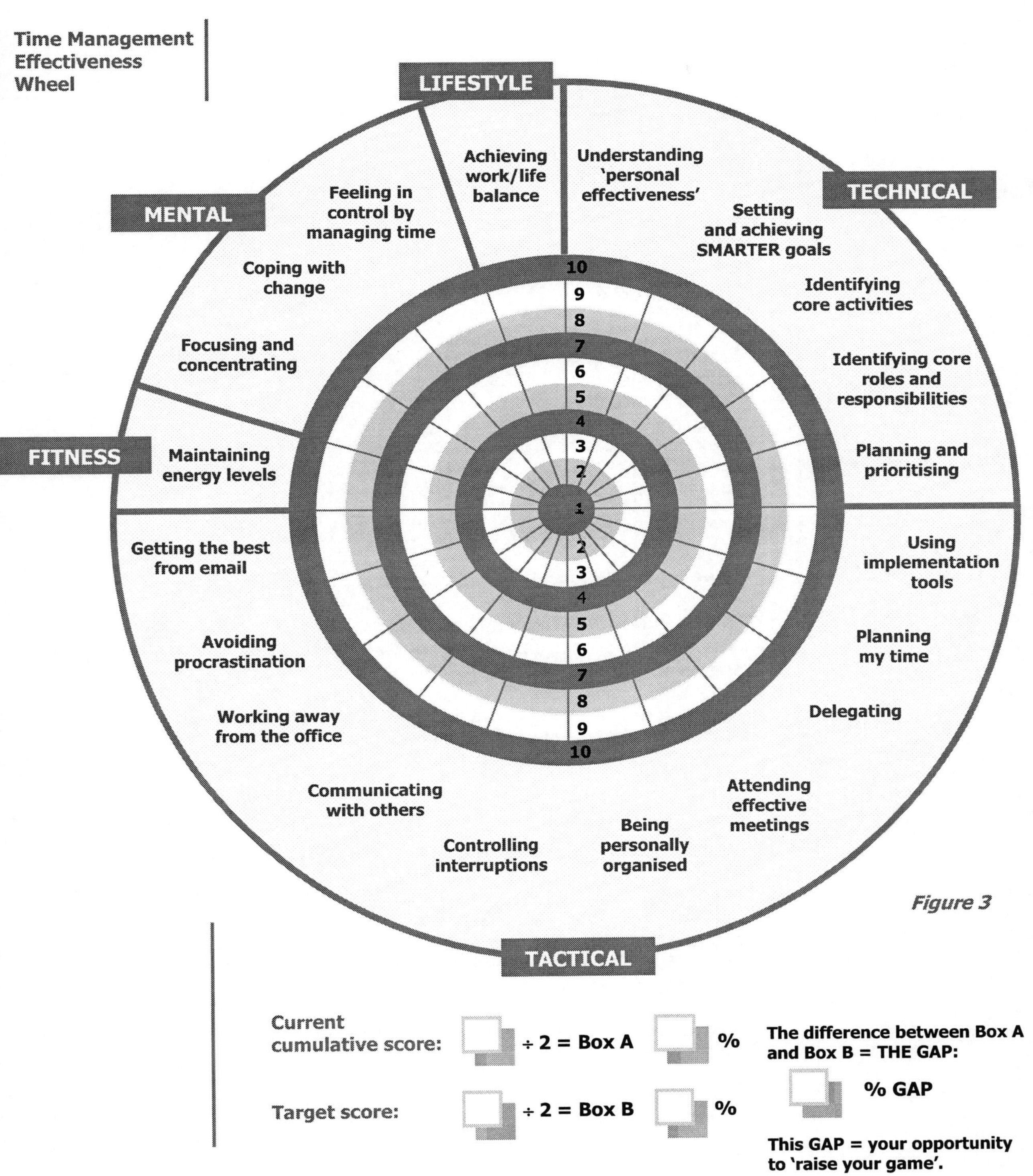
Time Management Effectiveness Wheel
LIFESTYLE
TECHNICAL
TACTICAL
FITNESS
MENTAL
Achieving work/life balance
Understanding 'personal effectiveness'
Setting and achieving SMARTER goals
Identifying core activities
Identifying core roles and responsibilities
Planning and prioritising
Using implementation tools
Planning my time
Delegating
Attending effective meetings
Being personally organised
Controlling interruptions
Communicating with others
Working away from the office
Avoiding procrastination
Getting the best from email
Maintaining energy levels
Focusing and concentrating
Coping with change
Feeling in control by managing time
10
9
8
7
6
5
4
3
2
1
2
3
4
5
6
7
8
9
10
Current cumulative score:
÷ 2 = Box A
%
Target score:
÷ 2 = Box B
%
The difference between Box A and Box B = THE GAP:
% GAP
This GAP = your opportunity to 'raise your game'.

Figure 3

Debriefing your Effectiveness Wheel

Method 1:
Working individually

Look at the scores that you have given yourself and ask why is it that some merit a score of 7 or 8, whilst others were only worthy of a 3, 4 or 5?

What you have done here is to review your existing performance. You have identified where things are working well and where things are working less well. If you can analyse each segment on the wheel and identify who, or what, is preventing you from attaining a higher score, then it is a short step to begin to plan what to do differently, in order to raise your game.

Use the Spreadsheet in Figure 4 to gather your thoughts about the proactive actions that you can take in each area. Notice that there are three columns headed 'Company', 'Department or Team' and 'Me'. These are meant to help you to identify where **you** think responsibility for bringing about change in this particular area lies. Put a tick in the appropriate column (you may choose to tick more than one), and notice as you go how often you tick the 'Me' column! Then add your action plan points to the rest of the sheet.

Method 2:
Working with a partner (colleague, peer, mentor or coach)

If you review the Effectiveness Wheel with someone else, you may find it useful for both of you to fill in a version of the wheel, so that you can do some reciprocal coaching.

In this process, you will need to decide who will be **Partner 1** and who will be **Partner 2**. **Partner 1** goes first and will simply talk through their Effectiveness Wheel. "This is how I scored myself and this is why I scored it as I did".

Partner 2's role will be to listen, to draw out and to get clarity from **Partner 1**. As **Partner 1** talks, **Partner 2** should encourage them to notice those areas where they think they could, or should, move their score forward.

Partner 2 will be supportive, but should aim to probe, dig and nudge in order to help **Partner 1** to identify what they need to do, how best they can go about it and who they will need to draw upon for support. The partner also has an important role to play in helping to establish a realistic time frame for action. Again, this can be captured on the Spreadsheet.

Having looked at one partner's wheel, both partners should switch roles and repeat the exercise.

Where does responsibility for bringing about change in each of these areas lie? Tick ✓ the box(es) as appropriate:	**Company?**	**Department or Team?**	**Me?**	**Actions**
1. Understanding personal effectiveness				
2. Setting and achieving SMARTER goals				
3. Identifying core activities				
4. Identifying core roles and responsibilities				
5. Planning and prioritising				
6. Using implementation tools				
7. Planning my time				
8. Delegating				
9. Attending effective meetings				
10. Being personally organised				
11. Controlling interruptions				
12. Communicating with others				
13. Working away from the office				
14. Avoiding procrastination				
15. Getting the best from email				
16. Maintaining energy levels				
17. Focusing and concentrating				
18. Coping with change				
19. Feeling in control by managing time				
20. Achieving work/life balance				

Figure 4

You are welcome to reproduce this sample pro-forma. Alternatively copies can be downloaded from http://www.stepsystem.co.uk/stepsystem-downloads.html

The three boxes

As you go through this thinking / discussion process, be aware that every issue you address will fit into one of three boxes – there are some things that you can **Change** by yourself (Box 1); some things that you can **Influence** (Box 2) – that is, things that you can change in partnership with other people (customers, colleagues, or with your team); and there are some things that you can do *absolutely* **Nothing** about (Box 3).

Most people find that they use 'I' language to discuss the things that they can change ("I can...", "I will..."); they use 'We' language to discuss things that they might achieve in collaboration with others ("We can...", "We will..."); and they use 'They' language to discuss things over which they feel there is little opportunity to affect change ("They should...", "They could...").

This simply reflects the extent to which they feel able to influence the implementation of the necessary change.

Rather than become stressed by the things that you cannot affect, focus on those areas where you can make a difference, ("I can change it" or "We can influence it").

Action plan

Having completed your scoring and thinking about the Effectiveness Wheel, decide what your next steps will be.

Do not try to change everything at once. Be realistic, have clear deadlines and set yourself for success.

Capture your current thinking below:

This exercise is worthwhile completing on a half yearly basis and will help you to consistently push at 'raising your game', while keeping abreast of changes taking place around you.

Chapter 1

Attitudes towards Time, Breaking Habits and Coming to Terms with Change

- Your personal timelines
- Find a bigger 'Yes!'
- Being busy versus being effective
- Goal setting, planning and proactivity
- Creating your own plan
- Raising your game
- Case Study 1
- Case Study 2
- Gaining focus
- Planning time
- Case Study 3
- Personal change
- Awareness, Awkwardness, Skill, Habit
- Case Study 4
- Encouraging change in others
- Dealing with change
- The three circles: knowledge, skill and desire
- Comfort zones

Your personal timelines

Time is a finite resource. We only get 24 hours in each day and, if the time is not spent wisely, we cannot put some on one side to save for use on another day!

The diagram below represents your lifeline.

0 represents the day that you were born and **+** represents the day that you die.

0 ———————————————————————————— **+**

Mark where you are on the line right now. (Most people try to get as close to the left hand end as they reasonably can!)

If you were to discover that you are actually ***much closer*** to the right hand end than you hoped:

- ☐ Would it affect **how** you chose to spend your time today, or this week?
- ☐ Would it affect **who** you chose to spend your time with?
- ☐ Would it affect **how** you behaved and **what** you communicated with those people?

It is likely that having less time would change your perspective and make you rather more selective in what you choose to do. Above all, having less time would give you strength (perhaps even the necessary excuse) to stop doing those things which, on reflection, are comparatively low in value and to focus instead on your core, important things.

Now that you have thought about it, does anything else strike you about **how** you would spend your time or **who** you would spend it with? Is there a sense that if you have so little time, you might begin to wish you had started doing some of the important things rather sooner?

Our supply of personal or discretionary time really is running out and (unfortunately) most people are actually much closer to the right hand end of the line than they would hope... and even then, a large tranche of whatever is left will be spent working, another tranche doing maintenance tasks and yet more simply watching television or sleeping...

Look again at the line. Where are you right now? How much time will be 'lost' to work or maintenance tasks? How much discretionary time do you really have left?

Most people have very little discretionary time to spend – wouldn't it be good to decide how you want to use it?

The way that people choose to spend their time on a daily basis is often a product of how much of it they perceive that they have available to them. Interestingly, some people who may drift or get pulled about by other people's agendas during normal worktime, find it easier to get focused and 'up-to-date' in the last few days before going on holiday, when they perceive that they 'have less time' and an obvious deadline.

Find a bigger 'Yes!'

Why should these few days be any different from 'normal' days? One overriding reason is that having a deadline by which they need to have cleared the desk or left the building helps them to say 'NO!', simply because they now have a bigger 'YES!'

Most people find it easier to leave work, a meeting or a training course when they have another commitment in place that they feel somehow excuses them:

"I'm sorry I have to leave, but it's my MBA ... it's my turn with the kids ... I have another meeting... I have a train to catch..."

This highlights one of the greatest benefits of planning ahead – prior planning means that you will always know the opportunity cost* of saying 'Yes'. Without this insight, it is much harder for most people to say 'No!'

Time flies... Have you noticed that sometimes when you are having a pleasurable experience and you want it to go on for ever, time seems to fly by?

Have you noticed that when you are bored or when you are waiting for something to begin, time seems to drag?

Have you noticed that it is sometimes easier to get focused on completing a task as the deadline gets closer?

With a greater sense of urgency comes an increased focus – perceived pressure is often a driver to get more done, in less time.

Time always runs at the same speed, but our attitude towards it changes and our attitude will affect the value that we can take from each unit of 'time currency' available to us.

---

* Opportunity cost is the cost of a lost opportunity when a choice is made. For example, if by choosing one particular product, you lose the chance to purchase another, the opportunity cost of your choice is the lost benefit of the item foregone. Opportunity cost can also be applied to time allocation. My family and I have a Saturday evening free, to do anything we want. We have decided either to go to the cinema or to go bowling. We decide to go bowling instead of to the cinema, so the opportunity cost of bowling on this occasion, is to not go to the cinema.

Effective Time Management

What does time management mean to you?

____

____

____

What is your mental image of someone who manages their time well? What is it that they do right?

____

____

____

Being busy versus being effective

In our modern world, it is not hard to be busy, but it is hard to be effective. Because of pressure of work, many people invest in tools and work hard to improve their existing systems and processes in the hope that they will become more organised and efficient, enabling them to deliver a greater volume of work.

Whilst this may have some logic, it is only a part of the story. What is the point of doing things in a faster, better, or more cost-effective way, if we are doing the wrong things?

Effective time management is about getting the most from today, so that we can achieve short-term targets, whilst positioning ourselves to be able to achieve long-term hopes and ambitions in the future, as well. It is a 'double whammy', worth striving for!

Goal-setting, planning and proactivity

The real battleground is best summed up as a three-stage process, often adopted by people who are truly successful.

These people:

- ❑ have a clear destination – a focus.
- ❑ have a route for the journey mapped out – a plan.
- ❑ spend time on the journey, and by avoiding getting side-tracked along the way, they proactively do what they have to do ... and if they are smart, they also review, so that they can learn lessons and improve the process, before refocusing and moving on.

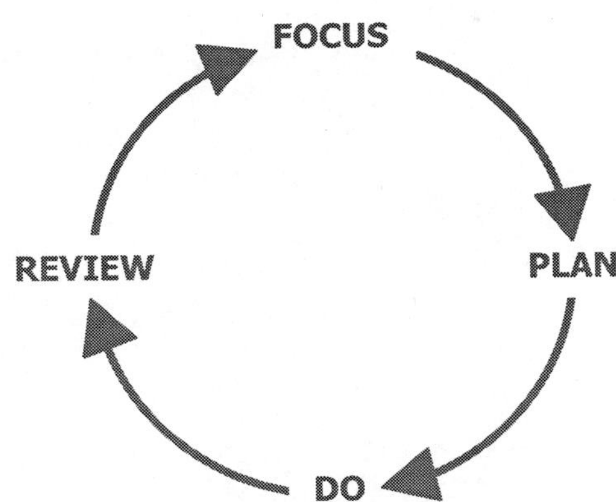

Figure 5

Creating your own plan

What is your focus in your job? What is it really about? What is your contribution to the business? Where do you add value?

____

____

____

Raising your game

In order to progress, both in our careers and in our lives as a whole, we need to apply our experience and intelligence and recognise that the skills that we have and the things that we have historically done, may not necessarily be the skills or actions that we need in order to move forward. To improve our performance does not require us to apply more time doing the same things; it requires us to find a *better* use of our time, sometimes adding new skills and actions to complement and perhaps replace our existing ones.

This model is as helpful with sports people as it is with business people. Both groups need to focus on raising their game. No matter how good they were last year the competition will have been watching and learning and are now snapping at their heels!

Case Study 1:

What are we in Business to do?

If you were to ask some of Britain's top boxers what they do, they might initially find it hard to answer, other than to say: "I am a boxer". They go to the gym. They work on their fitness, their technical skills, their mental attitude and do a whole bunch of generic things that define them as 'a boxer'. It is much easier for them to say "What I am..." than to explain "What I do..."

A consultant armed with a flipchart, a pen and a nudging technique, may help them to list the functional aspects of being a boxer: "We hit people... we jab... we learn to feint to the left and hit with the right... we get up more often than we get knocked down..."

A different question however, may help them to think tangentially. By asking them to identify what it is that the best performers in their field do well, to identify the things that these role models 'do right' – they may think of a different list, which could be recorded on a second flipchart.

They will notice that the real 'big boys' in boxing can fill a stadium. They sell their share of the tickets in order to get their share of the purse. They develop a media personality. They learn how to manage and manipulate the press. They develop business interests outside of boxing. They think of beginning to develop their careers to make themselves marketable in advance of when they no longer want or are able to fight...

Ask most boxers which flipchart list they spend most of their time on and they will say: "Flipchart 1" and, as a result, if they are not achieving everything that they want, the temptation will always be to go back to the gym and to work harder – they are unlikely to get to Flipchart 2, because they are too busy, being busy.

They would do well to realise that although they need to get the first list right before they can completely move on to the second, they need to work on both lists – and failing to do so will significantly limit their ability to be successful.

In the world of sport, even the best performers search consistently to find ways to leverage more from their performance and to raise their game, albeit by fractions of a percent. Over time, the opposition learns from them and may adopt their tactics themselves. In response, top performers continually work on their strengths, develop new skills or improve areas of perceived weakness, in order to keep moving forward.

Many of us do not achieve this clarity until we leave a job and hear ourselves say: "Well, of course, if I had my time again I would do things differently..."

One wonders where this fantastic insight comes from on our last day and, more importantly, what use it is to us now that we are leaving!

In order to improve time management skills, we need to achieve a clarity that can only come through raised awareness about what our job is <u>really</u> about, whilst we are still immersed in doing it!

To bridge the gap from where we are now to where we could or should be, it is possible to work proactively on any number of areas. It may be that we can leverage benefit by focusing on the team – (mentoring, coaching, delegating, driving PDPs and succession plans) or by focusing on leadership, communications or personal organisation. All of these, tackled in a positive and proactive way, will enable us to achieve more.

True maturity is not about using our success as an excuse to keep things the same; rather it should be a springboard to give us the confidence to recognise that this year we have the possibility of being **even** better than last year and that by leveraging opportunity and possibility, we can make some dramatic strides forward.

Many of us may have the same job title and receive a similar salary this year as we did last year, but the world in which we are expected to operate has moved on.

Most people are already working hard enough and the intelligent thing to do is to find ways to deliver more, by working SMARTER. Luckily, each year brings fresh knowledge and experience – and mature performers can use their experience as a catalyst for change – and not as an excuse to keep on doing what they are already doing!

Case Study 2:

"We're all fighting fires."

People who belong to the Fire Service are in the business of fighting fires. They have an ever growing demand on their scarce firefighting resources, and as a result need to be increasingly proactive in finding new and innovative ways to address their 'customers needs' – perhaps even preventing them from needing to call out the fire service in the first place.

Firefighters attend training courses to learn how to deal with new gases, chemicals or building techniques. They go into schools and colleges and teach young people about the dangers of starting fires. They inspect hospitals, offices, hotels and public buildings to ensure that each has the appropriate fire procedures in place.

Instead of doing any of these things, they could have argued that they do not have time for preventative activities, because they need to be responsive to their customers and cannot risk leaving the fire station, in case there is a fire. This feeling is recognisable to many people in business, who feel that they are too busy being customer-focused, or 'busy being busy,' to be able to really manage their time, to get around to getting organised, or to be truly proactive.

Firefighters are under so much pressure that they have to find innovative ways to work SMARTER and there are lessons to be learned from their approach. They have found, for example, that by analysing data, it is possible for all of the emergency services to plot the likelihood of an incident happening at any given location at any time. With this technology, they can predict the likely demand for their services, for example on a stretch of motorway with roadworks and a contra-flow system in place, perhaps on a bank holiday, in poor weather and at dusk.

The high likelihood of an incident happening means that they may choose to have vehicles and personnel on standby close at hand, waiting for a problem to develop. By working this example through they have discovered that when they deploy the resources of any of the accident services at a specific location in a high profile way, motorists slow down and perversely, the likelihood of an accident taking place is reduced!

So, the next logical step might be to ask: if simply having a parked vehicle can reduce the risk of accident, then does the vehicle need to be manned? To really push out the boundaries, could they even use dummy vehicles to give the illusion of a presence and so release both people and valuable equipment for proactive activity elsewhere, to be available on standby for some other emergency that cannot be predicted?

But here is the rub. Why do most firefighters join the profession in the first place? For many, it has to do with the adrenaline rush that they get from dealing with major emergencies. This is exactly the opposite of what an effective member of the fire service should be striving to spend their time on! Presumably, not many firefighters would have joined the brigade in the first place, if they had realised that their job was going to be about setting up dummy vehicles on motorway bridges!

This idea is not completely outlandish. Several police forces are currently trialling the idea of putting cardboard cut-outs of police officers in the back of cars in hotel car parks, to deter drive-by car thieves and are using decommissioned cars to show a 'police presence' when there are actually no officers in an area.

Firefighters and police officers are being asked to do different things in order to achieve their organisations' goals and some may resent it. Their feelings may be similar to their peers in industry, who find themselves responding to change by saying: "This isn't why I joined this company..."

Good time management – the foundation of effectiveness – is not about processing volume, or being busy. It is about keeping focused on the end goal and sub goals, prioritising what needs to be done and utilising a scarce resource – available time – in order to achieve them.

Gaining focus

If you want to look back at the end of this year and feel that you have been highly effective, what should you have spent your time doing?

What areas of work would you have focused on?

What areas of work would you have spent **less** time on than you do currently?

Which people would you have spent **more** time with than you do currently?

Which people would you have spent **less** time with than you do currently?

____

____

____

For most people, the time when they most need to plan coincides with the time when they have the least time to do it.

Planning time

How much time do you honestly have?

Time can be split into three main parts:

- ❑ Sold Time.
- ❑ Maintenance Time.
- ❑ My Time.

...and this can be represented very clearly on a pie chart, with the full circle representing a 24 hour day.

Figure 8

In this diagram, Sold Time is the time given by an individual to their employers in return for cash; Maintenance Time is used for shopping, cooking, ferrying the kids around; what's left (and this is how most people think of it) is called My Time.

If Sold Time is not well managed – and because there are no shortage of things to do, it is easily consumed – then obviously it will grow and something else has to give way. For most people, Maintenance Time is already pared down to a minimum and so what suffers, and what gives, is inevitably ... My Time!

Is that the outcome you would choose?

Case Study 3:

Putting out fires before they start

A small group of firefighters travelled from the south of England to a regional airport in the Midlands, where they took part in an exercise dealing with a simulated passenger plane crash-landing. Representatives of the police, the fire brigade, the ambulance service and other organisations all took part and together they dealt with the situation quickly and effectively.

However, the post-event debrief highlighted some issues. The organiser called together all the participants and began his session with an open question:

"Well, how did that go then?" To which one firefighter replied:

"Very well... if you live in the perfect world!" Warming to his theme, he went on:

"You seem to make so many assumptions... You seem to assume that if an aeroplane is travelling to this airport and it crashes, it will crash neatly beside Runway 2... We travelled up here last night on that mobile car park you call the M1 and it took us three hours to do the last 12 miles.

"So, what would happen if the plane didn't quite make it to the airport?

"What if it came down the other side of that huge traffic jam, near the power station, close to the factories, beside the hospital and the school?

"With the best will in the world, it would take firefighters from this station at least half an hour to get there..."

This was a major 'Aha' for the local commander, out of which he and his team began to develop a new strategy.

They decided that in future, if a plane was coming to the airport and it was in trouble, they would send half of their engines to wait for it beside the emergency runway (Runway 2) as they had always done, but they would send the other half of their engines to begin working their way through the traffic jam – **immediately**, without waiting for the plane to reach the airport. The idea being that if the distressed plane flew over them, they could turn around and follow it back in, but if it should come down the wrong side of the motorway, the wrong side of the road works and the traffic jams, near the power station the factories, the hospital and the school, then they would already be on their way to the scene of the crash.

In other words, they were beginning to engage with the crisis, even before it happened – true proactivity!

It seems that often the more people need to plan, the less likely they are to put time aside to do so. Most people accept that planning is a good idea, but have a million reasons why **they** cannot do it, in **their** job right **now**.

In common with any other business, firefighters need to be responsive to their customers' needs. They focus on using their scarce resources effectively, whilst accepting that by its very nature, their business is reactive.

Investing time in the kind of training exercise outlined above is key and, as with many other activities, it is not just having gone through the experience that matters, but the tangential learning that can come from the debrief – as with this case study, leading to improved time management, resource utilisation and overall effectiveness.

Failing to plan is like planning to fail. Finding 15 minutes a day, will make it more likely that the things most necessary for success arrive at the top of the task list and it is the things of least value that will not get done.

Personal change

In order to meet the challenges of our modern world, it might be useful to try to see the problems in a new way – move on from old beliefs like: "If it ain't broke don't fix it," and excuses like: "But that's the way we have always done it around here", because:

"If we always do what we have always done, we will probably get the results that we have always got".

Rosabeth Moss Kanter

If we think it is important to achieve different ends, it follows that we may need to meet the challenge in a different way.

"There is no point in trying to manage your time, unless you are willing to change the way you spend it"

In order to come to terms with change, it will be necessary to go through the 4 stages of:

- ❑ **Awareness**
- ❑ **Awkwardness**
- ❑ **Skill**
- ❑ **Habit**

Awareness

As with all developmental processes, it is essential to understand the starting point – the 'Where am I now?' The reason for completing the Effectiveness Wheel in the introduction and the question-and-answer segments throughout the rest of this book is simply to encourage this thought process.

Looking in the mirror and seeing ourselves as we really are is a good springboard to identifying where there is the opportunity or desire to move forward.

Awkwardness

Unfortunately, many people will identify that it is much easier to do the things that they have always done in the way that they have always done them than it is to go through the pain of change. There are lots of real or imagined opportunities to give up – the task will take longer, the results will not be as good and they may not be as proud of the outcomes – but these are all symptoms of awkwardness and giving in means that progress cannot be made.

Skill

Refining old skills or developing new ones can be incredibly satisfying, but in the early stages, there may be dissatisfaction with the quality, quantity or speed of output. Performance can only really peak when the performer knows that they are doing the right things, in the right way and have confidence in their own ability to deliver.

Habit

Persevering and finding a way to overcome the negative thoughts that often invade our head whilst we are going through the pain of change, will mean that the journey to developing a new set of skills (which with practice will become a habit) is well on its way, creating firm foundations for what you now choose to do.

At the outset of the discovery process, many people are 'unconsciously incompetent' – in other words, they lack skill or knowledge to do a specific task, but they are blissfully unaware of their short comings.

By raising their awareness, they become 'consciously incompetent' – they still lack the skill or knowledge to do a specific task, but now at least they are aware of their short comings!

Of course this is a dangerous stage – people feel as though things are getting worse and it is this that sometimes prompts people on training courses to say: "I wish that I had not come on this course, because I now realise how much I have to do."

My response is usually to point out that they always had this much to do; it's just that they had not realised it before!

Perseverance at this stage is key and will lead to the individual becoming 'consciously competent' – when they can generally perform the task to a good standard, but they may be slow, they may make some errors and completion still demands an investment of time and brain power.

Eventually however, they will emerge on the other side, 'unconsciously competent' – able to complete the task and unable to remember a time when it did not come to them as a natural skill!

The challenge is that we do not know what we do not know and the trick is to find any way that we can to open up our horizons.

Eradicating bad habits, applying creative thinking techniques and coming to terms with positive change are all necessary stages in enabling individuals to release and leverage their latent potential. This is also particularly important to understand for anyone who is interested in developing the performance of others and is possibly a central requirement for every one of us – manager or not.

Case Study 4:

Learning to drive

Awareness

Most people can work out for themselves how useful it would be to be able to drive long before they hit the legal age. If they live in a place with poor public transport, the possibility of having their own car offers both freedom and independence.

They can visualise themselves driving along, perhaps wearing shades, with the wind in their hair, able to do and go wherever they want...

In the UK, although the minimum legal driving age is 17, many people begin to look forward to being able to drive long before their 17th birthday and, as it is such an important landmark in their lives, it does not take much for their awareness to be raised.

Most 17-year-olds can visualise the stage they expect to get to and assume that it is just a formality for them to get through their driving test.

Before their first lesson, they have the confidence that comes with innocence – and the certainty that comes with youth.

Exploring the root of the confidence may reveal that initially the learner driver thinks that driving must be relatively easy – after all, their parents or grandparents are able to do it and they have been quite able to offer comment and advice to their elders from the back seat for years!

Awkwardness

Arriving for their first lesson, they soon discover that they are in fact stepping into a completely alien world.

Sitting behind the wheel, they find that everything looks very different.

Perhaps for the first time, it dawns upon them just how many things they now have to think about and be responsible for.

These first few moments for the learner driver can be truly nerve-racking.

Turning on the engine, managing the clutch, being aware of others, as well as themselves, are all incredibly daunting and the multi-tasking required can be difficult to co-ordinate.

Skill

Having budgeted for a couple of quick 'exam-passing technique' lessons, the aspiring driver may well discover that in reality they need several more.

After these additional lessons, lots of practice and possibly a few tests, they arrive at a standard where they have really begun to develop sufficient skill to be able to justify gaining a licence.

Habit

Most people would recognise, however that it is only through the probationary period that true driving skills evolve. With the opportunity for more practice and varied experience, enhanced skills and confidence are developed as a result of which, finally, good and safe driving becomes a habit.

There is however a problem with this. It is widely recognised that most people can identify bad driving in others, whilst believing themselves to be both considerate and safe...

... very few people feel the need to take advanced driving qualifications, because they know that they are developing as a driver anyway. Very soon after passing their test, they discover that their 'lightning reactions' mean that they do not have to worry about speed restrictions or driving too close to the car in front. They find that they can steer with their little finger, whilst eating a sandwich or reading a map and because of their exceptional skills, they can even change the CDs, (which are stored under the passenger seat), whilst undertaking on the inside lane of the motorway...

In truth, many people might find that within a few years of passing their test, they would find it hard to pass it were they to take it again, as so many bad habits have crept in.

This experience is in many ways akin to the step that some people make from being a team member to becoming a Supervisor or Manager. They have been playing their functional role happily – watching their boss from the side lines, doing what they do and then one day, somebody says: "You have been around long enough; you know the job, why don't you take over the running of the team?"

Just like the aspiring driver, they are likely to be about to get a rude awakening, as they make the journey through awareness to habit, discovering along the way that there is more to the job than there appears to be and that it is definitely not as easy as it looks! In fact, there is a lot to think about.

When addressing change, we should probably visit the 4-stage Awareness, Awkwardness, Skill, Habit model, twice.

Visit 1 Raised awareness will help us to see things as they really are and by going through the pain of change – and keeping going when things feel uncomfortable – we will arrive at a new stage of understanding, where the skills that we assimilate enable us to move forward, doing the right things.

Visit 2 We need to check that, unlike the learner driver, the habits that we have are deeply embedded and that we are not contaminated by shortcuts and cheats which, if they are allowed to creep in, will mean that as time passes we are not only not as good as we used to be, but that we stand no chance of becoming as good as we might be!

Encouraging change in others

We do not need our people to be as good as us – we need them to be better!

It is important to get a clear picture of what it is that we want people to do and that we make a point of recognising and rewarding the 'right' behaviour.

It is easy as a manager to delegate consistently to the person who delivers, in preference to the person who does not, (or who is high maintenance), in the same way that it is tempting not to bother to ask kids to tidy their bedroom, to wash the car or to mow the grass when all of their early attempts are so ineffective and frustrating.

Do not be tempted to redo, or to do it yourself next time – persevere! Set clear, reasonable targets, facilitate success and go out of your way to catch the performer doing something right. Set the goal, help them score the goal, help them to celebrate the goal and you will begin to create proven goal scorers! (See page 64.)

Dealing with Change

Managers and employees can see change as being a huge threat or an exciting opportunity – but one thing is certain, change is inevitable – the choice of how to act, or react to it, however, lies with the individual.

The task of business leaders is to set direction, while the role of individual managers is to communicate that direction and to build the momentum needed through their own focus and enthusiasm for change. Their understanding of the current needs of the business, and their continued commitment and enthusiasm to bringing about change, are essential.

The three circles: knowledge, skill and desire

A real skill for managers is to get people to want to bother to go through the pain of change, and in order to cope with change, people need clarity. Knowing 'what' they need to do, along with having the appropriate skills, the 'how', will set them off in the right direction. To be successful, they also need the third ingredient – 'desire'.

Many organisations manage two out of three. Take, for example, an organisation that is filled with uncertainty. The people in the organisation may know how to do their job and they may want to do it, but if they are no longer clear about what it is that the business expects from them in their 'brave new world', they may well be frozen into inactivity.

Alternatively, imagine a business where people understand what is expected of them – they feel the pressure and they really want to do their best, but they lack the technical knowledge or skill. It is very hard for them to achieve as they would like and the most difficult thing is that they actually know how badly they are performing.

And what about the third option? Have you ever dealt with an organisation where it is quite clear that people know what it is that they have to do and they have the skills and experience to do it, but for some reason they really cannot be bothered?

True effectiveness and indeed good habits exist when the three circles of knowledge, skill and desire overlap.

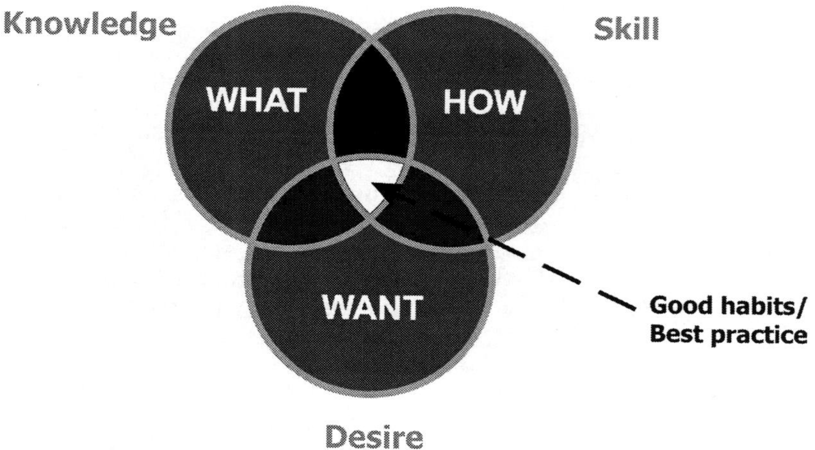

Figure 9

Helping people to know **what** they should do and **how** they should go about it and then finding a way to inject them with energy and enthusiasm to **want** to go through the pain is a business imperative and is central to achieving personal or team effectiveness.

Comfort zones

Doing the things that we have always done and failing to strive for improvement keeps us in the **Comfort Zone.**

We feel safe, at ease and in control, but it may also feel a little dull and unadventurous.

Pushing at the limits of the Comfort Zone can take us into the Learning or Stretch Zone – an area filled with opportunity and possibility.

People who are reluctant to change, sometimes confuse the Stretch Zone with the Stress Zone, where the additional pressures actually become counterproductive and prevent them from making real progress or from accessing their latent potential.

In the light of the above, how can you change what you do currently to raise your effectiveness in the future?

____

____

____

To be focused on being effective means proactively deciding what to do and (more importantly) what not to do! We need a mix of clarity, strategy and proactivity – and to exercise choice over our own attitudes and behaviours.

In our modern World, it is easy to be busy, but it is much harder to be effective! Choosing to do the right things right, is key.

"The world is moving so fast these days that the man who says it can't be done is generally interrupted by someone doing it."

Harry Emerson Fosdick

Chapter 2

Current Methods and Tools

- Deciding what to do
- Tools
- Case Study 5
- Case Study 6
- Alternative types of To-do lists
- Diaries
- Case Study 7
- Diary use
- Find 15 minutes a day to plan
- Finding the right tools

Deciding what to do

Think about how you operate on a day-to-day basis. How do you decide what you are going to do and when you are going to do it? Different people use different methods, depending on their job function and the extent of their management responsibilities.

People driven by goals, objectives and competency

Some people take the corporate vision, which is broken down into departmental goals or targets and use competencies and their job description to work with their manager to develop their objectives.

These objectives can then be broken down further into a quarterly or monthly game plan and key performance indicators, which enable them to prioritise both their time and activity.

These people are often driven by the important.

People driven by daily plans

Some people like to begin to think about their day ahead on the journey into the workplace, fitting things to do around already arranged meetings and existing commitments.

These things are loosely linked to 'doing their job'. When they arrive at work, they begin to work on those things which they think are the most pressing today.

These people are driven by the pre-booked and by the urgent.

People driven by "to do" lists and emails

Other people arrive at work and simply 'join in'.

Their work comes from conversation, yellow stickies on their PC screen, incoming phone calls and emails. They tend to pick up from where they got to yesterday and add new things, as they materialise, to their 'to do' list.

These people are driven by whatever gets their attention and are reactive.

List the thinking and written processes that **you** go through on a daily or weekly basis in order to be able to say: "I have a plan and I know it is the right plan."

Processes:

____

____

____

____

____

____

Look at your list. Have you written the processes that you go through, or have you listed some of the tools that you use to deliver the processes?

Most people actually find it quite difficult to define the thinking and recording that they do in order to arrive at a plan, but find it much easier to list the tools that they use to implement it! It is far less important to spend time choosing one tool above another, than it is to understand what needs to be done – a decision which must come first – after which it is then imperative to find the most appropriate tool(s) to carry out implementation – a choice that is completely subjective.

Almost everyone has access to a PC, but whether they get full benefit from it depends on the extent to which they have unpacked it, plugged it in, turned it on, put some good 'stuff' in and got some good 'stuff' out. Very few people can honestly claim to use the full potential of their PC.

It does not matter which tools people actually choose. There is no point trying to persuade a 'technophobe' to use a hand-held electronic system, or a 'techno-luster' to use a paper system. They will both need to find the best method to suit them, which will depend on their personal preferences, their job role, their history, their working environment and their budget.

Tools

Use Figure 10 below to list the tools that you use and identify the strengths and weaknesses of each.

What tools do you use?	What are the strengths and weaknesses of each?		
Tools	**Strengths**	**Weaknesses**	**Actions**

Figure 10

Case Study 5:

The mobile phone

John had a mobile phone supplied by his employers, so that he could improve his communications.

He had his mobile number printed on his business cards and headed paper and gave it out to his customers and colleagues. He finds that if he is out and about and he has a spare five minutes, he can use the phone to check if anyone needs to contact him.

Unfortunately, people use several other means of communicating with him as well and he not only has to check his mobile phone for voice and text messages; he also has to check back at the office with his PA, his voicemail, his answering machine, the departmental message book, his emails and faxes, and so on, in case anyone has tried to contact him by other means.

He has found that rather than improving his communications, his mobile phone has actually become *yet one more* place for people to leave him messages and *one more* medium through which he can be disturbed. It can actually contribute to him being less efficient.

John also finds that other people call him when it suits them and that as a result his working day is stretching. His boss has a long journey to and from the office and likes to call him out of office hours 'to catch up'; he has customers who work out of different geographical time zones and who call him on his mobile, because 'the land-line was on voice mail' and he finds that on days off, at weekends and on holiday people still call him and get through, as he needs his phone to be switched on, because he is expecting a call from family or friends.

Had he thought in advance, John might have chosen not to give out all his contact points quite so readily. As a result he would have had fewer places to check for messages.

He chose to have a mobile phone so that he could make outgoing calls and proactively respond to all of the other mediums that already exist. He could consider not giving out his number or have it switched to answer phone more frequently (with a good quality message, nudging callers towards when he will be available, i.e. during working hours, on working days), so that **he** can decide when he wants to be disturbed.

John might also like to invest in a personal phone, so that he can switch off his work phone and allow his private communications to carry on when he is not at work and vice versa.

Case Study 6:

To-do lists

Peter finds it useful to make 'to do' lists and sometimes he has several on the go at the same time. He knows that by dumping his thoughts down on paper he is able to ensure that he will not forget what he needs to do.

Sometimes however, Peter finds he has created what he calls a '36-hour to-do-today list' and having worked hard all day, he feels despondent because the list gives him a clear overview of all those things he still has not got around to doing!

The real reason for using lists is to clear the brain of the million-and-one things that would otherwise be held there. If we are certain that we will be reminded of them when we review the list, it will enable us to 'forget' them in the short term and give full attention to the things that are actually being done at the time.

A 'to do' list gives overview, enables prioritisation and reminds us to feel good about what we have done. Unfortunately, people like Peter simply begin to work from the top of the list, or they do the things that they like best, or which are easiest, first. As a result, they find that it is the same important, longer term, proactive tasks that get left until the next day or the day after...

Some people play games. They like to tick off the things that they have done, so that they can feel good. They then come back later and cross them out as well. A double whammy! Sometimes, they even find that they have done a job that was not on the list, so they write it down, tick it and then cross it out!

Never use 'a rolling list'. Always make a new list daily and recognise that if some things have not been done today, the moment may have passed. Look for the opportunity to just cross these out – proactively decide not to do them!

Alternative types of To-do lists

- ❑ **'Forget for now' list** – this is a great place to dump down things that occur to you that are not appropriate right now.

You can use these during meetings or whenever you get an idea washing around in your brain that is preventing you from thinking about or doing the things that should be concerning you at that moment.

Many people keep one of these beside the bed, as a place to jot down thoughts which might otherwise prevent them from getting to sleep. Gather these together and periodically check whether any of these random ideas have any life to them and can be developed.

- ❑ **A 'gap-filler' list** – Another really good variant of a 'to do' list is a 'gap-filler' list, (see Chapter 9). Whenever you come across something that you need to remember to do, but which does not need to be done right now, add it to the list.

Put a date in the deadline column by when it must be done. You can use this list to delay tasks until they are actually necessary – and with some tasks, if you leave them long enough either your plans change or the tasks no longer appear important enough to do – in either case you have not wasted time keeping yourself busy doing little things!

It takes a moment to check the list every day to spot those tasks that are close to deadline, whilst others with longer to run can be used as the basis for a 'standby list', to fill odd moments of time here and there – gaps between appointments, waiting for a meeting to start and so on.

This kind of tool makes it possible to tie up loose ends. There is insufficient time to do everything, so it is important to focus on the important things and to see the little things for what they are – fantastic gap-fillers!

Diaries

There are many diary formats. Four of the most common are diaries that give:

- ❑ a day to a view
- ❑ a week to a view
- ❑ a month to a view
- ❑ a year to a view.

Increasingly, people may use a mix of paper or electronic (desk-based and handheld) systems. They are also likely to use different formats and mediums for different parts of their life.

Case Study 7:

Paper and electronic diaries

Imagine that Peter and John have a meeting. They have a customer-supplier relationship and Peter has travelled from Bristol to Leeds for this meeting. They find that for some reason that they are running out of time (i.e. one of them needs to be somewhere else!) and so they agree to meet again at a later date.

How do they decide when they could next both make a meeting?

A common method is to reach for their electronic or paper diaries and compare notes, until they find a matching space. Unless they both have electronic diaries that automatically synchronise with their other systems, they are potentially heading for trouble.

Peter has his weekly diary with him (a print out of his 'journey plan'). He offers the earliest gaps that he has, until they find one that John can match.

Anyway, before confirming Peter thinks that he will need to check with his PA back in his office (where he has a day-to-a-page desk diary) that he is still free on that date. Like many people he has found that the more senior he has got in the organisation, the less control he seems to have of his own diary.

Increasingly, Peter finds that his diary fills up with appointments with other people and that tasks that he needs to complete in his own job have to fit into the gaps around the edges.

He has now booked a new two-hour meeting, but has not thought through that it will take out a huge chunk of his day, because he has to travel from Bristol to Leeds.

Perhaps he should question the alternatives:

- ❑ Does he need to travel?
- ❑ Could he invite John to come to him?
- ❑ What other mediums of communication would be acceptable to both parties?
- ❑ Could they have used their time at this meeting more effectively and avoided the need for a second?

Most importantly of all, Peter has not considered the consequences of having given away his time so easily. What will he not be able to do because he has chosen instead to spend another day meeting with John? He has no idea.

Peter's business has an open diary policy and everyone at senior level is expected to keep their Outlook calendar up to date. As Peter does not use a PDA that synchronises remotely, he has to update manually when he returns to the office, or ask his PA to do it for him.

When he calls to let her know about his planned meeting with John he is concerned that he might discover that his PA had already booked him out for a meeting – space in his diary is often perceived by his colleagues as being 'free' time, up for grabs because he is not busy; if they need a meeting, they tend to just get his PA to book him out. Peter feels that he is being treated like a resource; like a meeting room or a data projector, he is something to be 'booked' to suit others needs. He also begins to realise that his priorities are increasingly being established for him by others, who are deciding how and where he spends his most valuable resource, his personal time.

It also occurs to Peter that he is not sure of his family and social commitments on the afternoon and evening of his proposed meeting with John. He has the information, of course, but these sorts of bookings (attending clubs and societies, transporting children, parent's evenings, etc.) tend to go on the monthly calendar on the cork-board in the kitchen at home. He will find it hard to travel to Leeds and be back for an evening commitment. Clearly he needs to check...

Finally, he thinks that it would also be useful to look at the office wall chart and make sure that none of his team are away, or on training courses in the week of this planned meeting because if they are, he will need to man the help desk...

Like many people, Peter uses more than one sort of planning tool, because he is involved in different sorts of planning. He needs short-term detail and long-term overview and the problem can be that his planning tools cover different parts of his life and are geographically split. It is not surprising that sometimes he is overbooked, misses appointments, or has to stretch himself.

Several days after making his appointment with John, Peter is sitting at his desk and his boss asks him if he is 'free' on the 4th June. Peter checks his diary and has no problem telling his boss that he is in fact busy (because he has a prior engagement with John). On this occasion, it is easy to say 'No' to the boss, because he has a bigger 'Yes' already in place.

Now, imagine that Peter had never met with John. Let's re-run the film. The boss asks Peter if he is 'free' on the 4th June. Peter's diary is completely blank for that day so far ahead and he hears himself answering that he is 'free all day' – giving the impression that he was going to come to work and do some golf putting practice and a couple of Suduko quizzes. Actually this space in his diary represents a rare and wonderful occasion when he would have had some time to get on with the proactive aspects of his job – had he planned them in... and he has just blithely given the time away!

The boss then asks Peter to attend a sales conference on his behalf in Newcastle.

In the early hours of the 4th June, as Peter drives to Newcastle, he asks himself why, once again, he has been picked on to do this sort of task, when he has a million-and-one things to do back at his desk. The answer is simple. Going to Newcastle got a booking in his diary and once again, doing his job did not...

.. and sadly, he has only himself to blame!

There are a few simple steps that Peter could take to protect himself. He should:

- ❑ identify the important things that he needs to do in his job and then book meetings with himself in his diary when he will work on these tasks, before anyone else comes along with an alternative.
- ❑ protect these planned meetings with himself, just as aggressively as he would protect a business appointment with a customer, a supplier or a complete stranger.

This is particularly important in a company that uses a computer-based group diary. Often, because ours is such a meetings culture, a space in the diary is assumed to be a chunk of time when an individual is 'doing nothing' and is available.

Peter should:

- ❑ block out time in his diary that is not yet allocated – but which he is likely to need, so that it is not available for others to grab.
- ❑ establish patterns with his PA and his colleagues of when he would and would not like to be available to meet with them – it may suit him to have fewer well structured meetings at certain points or on certain days of the week, than to allow them to fill his diary at random.

Diary use

Many people use their diaries back to front. They use them to book out their time, with others filling it with meetings and events, and then they try to squeeze the things that they have to do into the gaps around the edges.

Good practice for diary use:

- ❑ Put in your holidays and days off.
- ❑ Put in your intended daily start and finishing times.
- ❑ Put in the regular (scheduled) tasks and commitments.
- ❑ Notice how much space is left. Think through, what else do you need to do to move forward in your job?
- ❑ Plan those things into the diary next – then, and only if you have to, allow public access.

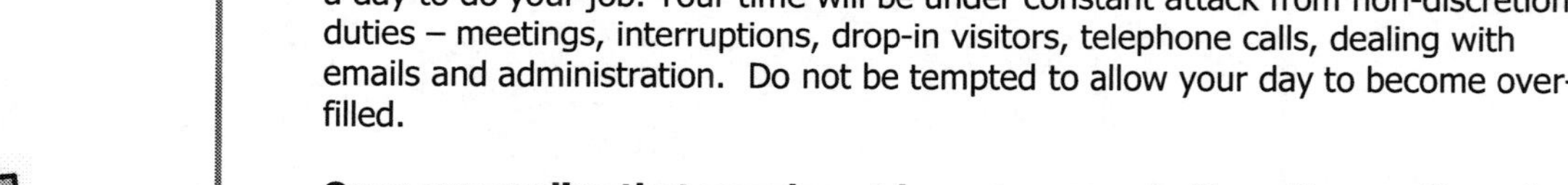
Be realistic with your diary planning. Recognise that you do not have eight hours in a day to do your job. Your time will be under constant attack from non-discretionary duties – meetings, interruptions, drop-in visitors, telephone calls, dealing with emails and administration. Do not be tempted to allow your day to become over-filled.

Once you realise that you do not have very much discretionary time, it becomes increasingly important to ensure that you spend the time that you *do* have doing those things that will leverage most benefit for *you*.

A daily planning format, similar to Figure 11 below, will make it much more likely that your time will be spent doing the right things.

Day **Date**

Important Today

07:00		
07:30		
08:00		
08:30		
09:00		
09:30		
10:00		
10:30		
11:00		
11:30		
12:00		
12:30		
13:00		
13:30		
14:00		
14:30		
15:00		
15:30		
16:00		
16:30		
17:00		
17:30		
18:00		
18:30		
19:00		
19:30		
20:00		
20:30		

Key Tasks	✓

Other Tasks	✓

☎	✉		✓

Figure 11

The things that we don't plan to do, we might as well have planned not to do – the outcome is the same. Get into your own diary before anyone else does!

What proactive process can you apply in order to decide how to spend your time each day?

What tools can you use to support this? Do you need to invest in new ones, or is it more important to address the way that you use the ones that you currently have in order to get enhanced value from them?

Find 15 minutes a day to plan

If you could find 15 minutes a day to plan and prepare, there is a much greater chance that the time available would be spent in the most appropriate way.

If you work a 220-day year, 15 minutes a day that are used to think and plan would equal a 7-day investment of your time. However, the potential pay-back and benefits in terms of doing the right things right could be phenomenal.

How can you generate 15 minutes extra per day?

What could you do more of, or less of?

What could you do differently, or not at all?

What could you do more quickly, or with more enthusiasm?

What could you do less well, or just well enough?

What could you do 'right first time', or to avoid hold-ups and bottle necks?

What could you stop doing, or find other people to do?

What could you do to develop other people, or to devolve your responsibilities to them?

What additional support do you need from your boss or from your colleagues in order to use your time more effectively?

Finding the right tools

Choosing the right tools and using them to their full potential, demands an investment of time.

There are so many tools available that it is impossible for one person to diagnose for another which they should use in order to help them to plan and to be organised. This is why our approach to time management focuses on good practice and sound principles of effectiveness and, once those are clear, encourages people to find the means of implementation which fits best with their approach, job and lifestyle.

Many businesses lay down some initial parameters by establishing corporate norms – via CRM, with policy about journey plans and open diary access – but generally businesses are most interested in **what** is achieved, often at the expense of the **how**...

Both organisations and individuals can make the mistake of thinking that the more expensive the tools the more efficient the user and the more effective the outcome – this is definitely not always the case!

Many paper systems are billed as being results-oriented planning tools – but they are often used as very expensive diaries. In the same way, many PDA's* are at best electronic diaries and contact books – they help people to fill their time, but rarely contribute much to supporting the clarifying process of **how** best to spend it.

People are at such different stages on the effectiveness journey and we at Step System work with all extremes – those who have clarity and focus and are very organised, some who are at the leading edge of technology (the early adopters who love to use innovative tools and techniques), and some who are completely haphazard in their approach and who do not even use a diary.

These people have different starting points, approaches, experiences and preferences, and their jobs and lifestyles have incredibly diverse requirements. Whilst there is an element of 'horses for courses', many people do have the 'head room' and the opportunity to raise their game by thinking about and developing the tools that they use to organise themselves and to implement the plan.

---

* PDA – Personal Digital Assistant is a term for any small mobile hand held device that provides computing and information storage retrieval capabilities for personal or business use, often for keeping schedule calendars and address book information handy.

Many people and businesses invest in new tools in an attempt to improve their time management. The benefits of this are negligible, unless individuals can decide 'what' they want to achieve and understand 'how' to use the tools to help them to achieve it. Investing in tools is not enough.

In the information age, as communication and information flow has been fuelled by the development of electronic tools, we should ask ourselves what is the point of doing things faster, if we are doing the wrong things?

It is only by applying intelligence and really working the tools that we have that anything like full value can be taken.

Have you got the right tools? If you have, what can you do to get even more value from them?

____

____

____

Have you got the right tools? If no, what alternative tools should you investigate and begin to use?

____

____

____

Chapter 3

Goals

- Becoming results oriented
- Goals
- Case Study 8
- Case Study 9
- High quality, SMART(ER) goals
- Case Study 10
- Case Study 11
- Goal setting – 3 years back and 3 years forward
- Recording and checking goals
- Goal Recording Pro-forma
- Act as if!
- Focus on it, dream it, plan it, do it!
- Case Study 12
- The first 100 days
- Your 80th birthday party
- Learning from Alice!
- Case Study 13
- Setting goals with a partner
- Setting goals with a family

Becoming results oriented

People who are successful tend to go through three stages:

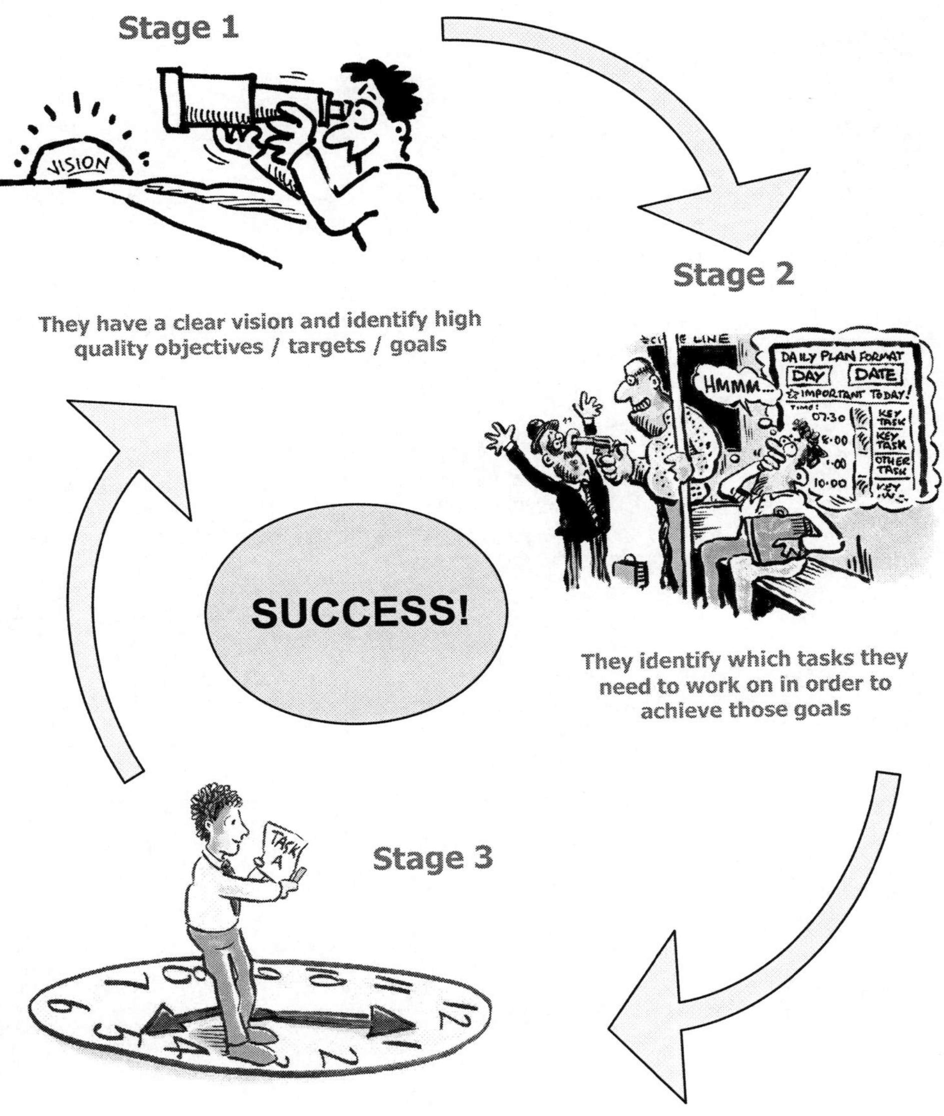

They spend time on those tasks

Figure 12

In essence, this means that successful people tend to focus on the three core skills of goal-setting, planning and proactivity. They decide upon their destination, they plan the best route to get there and they jolly well spend time on the journey!

Goals

The first and most important stage in becoming effective is to have clear goals and objectives.

What is a goal? (Brainstorm as many definitions as possible).

____

____

____

____

____

____

Many people come to realise that the term 'goal' could be used equally to describe things that they want to achieve in the short term (i.e. by 3 o'clock today), or in the longer term (i.e. by the time I retire). It might also be used to describe huge, potentially overwhelming things, or small stepping-stones, a component part in a much bigger success.

In sport, it is common for athletes to think in terms of three broad categories of goals. These are:

- ☐ **Dream Goals**
- ☐ **Performance Goals**
- ☐ **Process Goals**

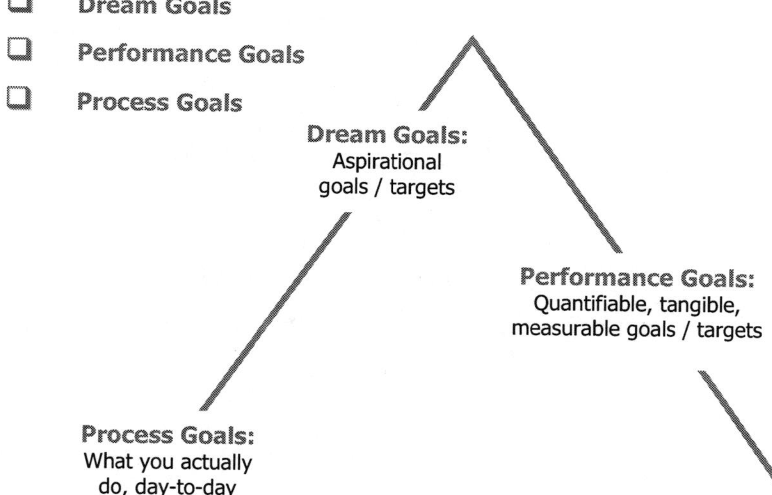

Figure 13

Athletes do not allow themselves to have too many goals or to have goals that conflict. They have focus and consistently question the opportunity-cost (see page 21) of everything that they do. In other words, they question whether the payoff is worth the investment.

A top athlete has a dream goal

This is a 'hazy vision' of a state of being, at some stage in the future when they will have 'arrived' or 'achieved success' and is often couched in terms of their 'being World Champion', or having 'got to the Olympics', or 'represented my country'.

It is often emotional and **always** motivational.

It represents the burning desire that keeps on driving them forward.

But how will they get to take part in the dream?

Usually they have to hit the right qualifying times, in the right qualifying events, on the right qualifying days.

If they hit enough of these tangible, quantifiable, measurable performance targets, then they get a chance to live the dream.

So, how do they achieve these performance targets?

Normally, they have to go through a process.

They consistently make choices to do certain things and, just as importantly, they choose **not** to do others.

They have to get up at a certain time, run X number of miles, do X hours in the gym, and travel X miles so that they can work with the best coaches and so on...

If they achieve enough of these process goals, they are in a great position to achieve their performance targets and the door starts to open on their dream.

- ❑ **Businesses also often have a dream goal** – this equates best with the corporate vision statement.
- ❑ **They have quantifiable / tangible performance targets** – these are departmental, team or personal goals.
- ❑ **They have process goals** – the things that have to be done on a day-to-day, week-to-week basis, if the performance targets and ultimately the dream are to be achieved.

Individuals in business, if they are results-oriented, can use the same structure to identify the things that they need to do to achieve their own definition of success.

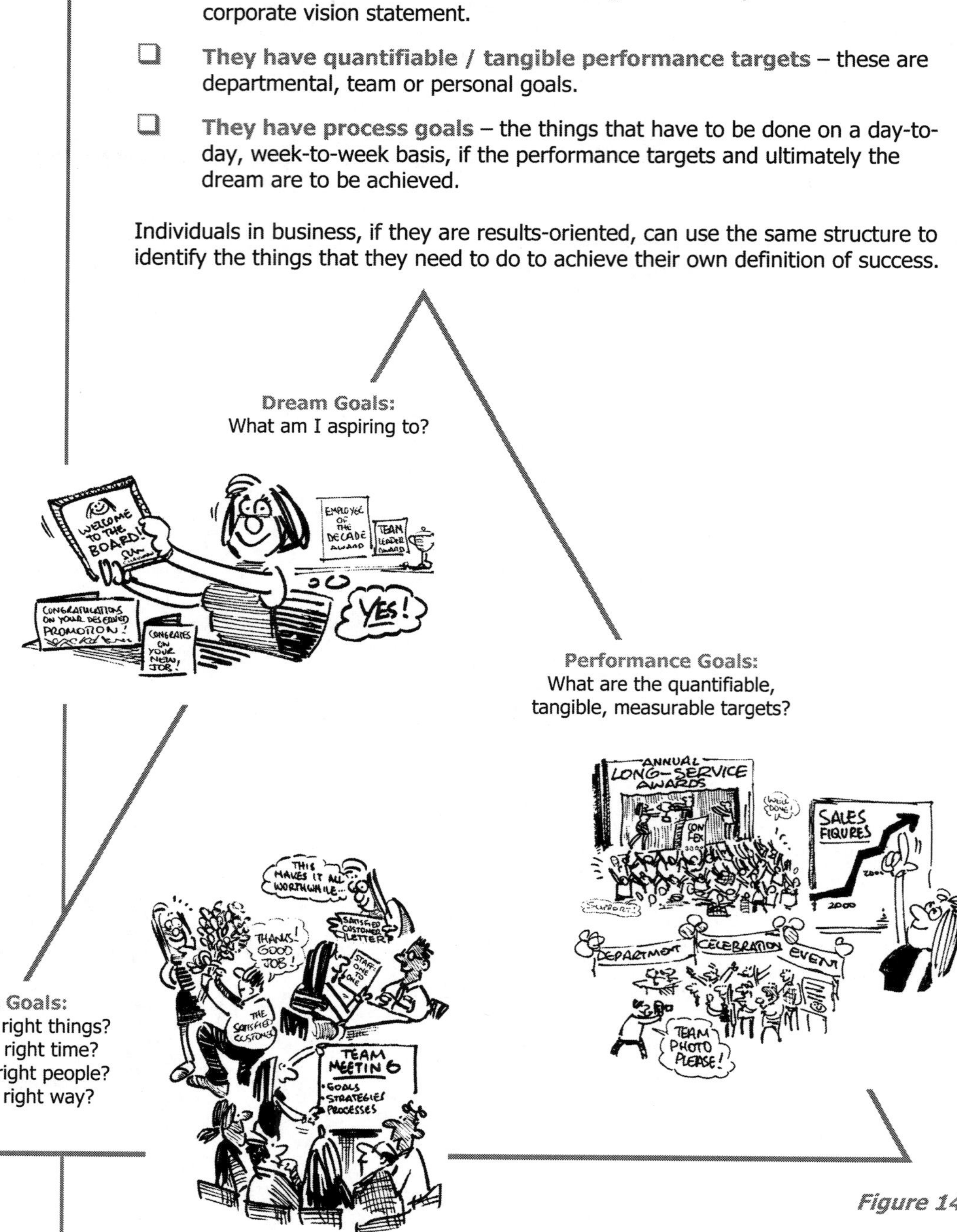

Figure 14

What are the benefits of having goals?

____

____

____

____

____

____

Case Study 8:

Making a positive decision to do nothing

For many years, Tony felt that he ought to learn to speak French. He would do nothing about it, but every year without fail, he would go to the South of France with his family and they would tell him that his idea of speaking French was to shout louder. Tony would respond by saying that he guessed he really 'ought' to learn to speak French... and when would he think of it next? Probably next time he was in the South of France, when, once again, he would be given the opportunity to look at himself and reconfirm his view of himself as a complete failure – being caught out by yet one more thing he has not done.

Eventually, Tony got results-oriented and goal-focused and he became much clearer about the business that he was in. This really helped him to decide what he was committed to and what he was not committed to. Finally, in France he changed the tape after several years and declared that he had **no intention** of learning to speak French, because he was not in the business of doing that. Simultaneously, he gave himself permission not to feel guilty about what he had not done, but instead to take confidence and strength by reminding himself of all of the proactive, worthwhile and fundamentally important things (to him, his business, his family) that he *had* done.

By deciding not to learn French, Tony was in a much better position than he had been for the last several years. Although he still could not speak French, he no longer felt guilty about not doing it!

One of the most powerful decisions anyone can make is to release themselves from the baggage of 'oughts', 'coulds', 'shoulds' and 'will do one days' by identifying the important things that they are absolutely committed to and giving their focus and energy to those things instead.

Case study 9:

Getting clarity

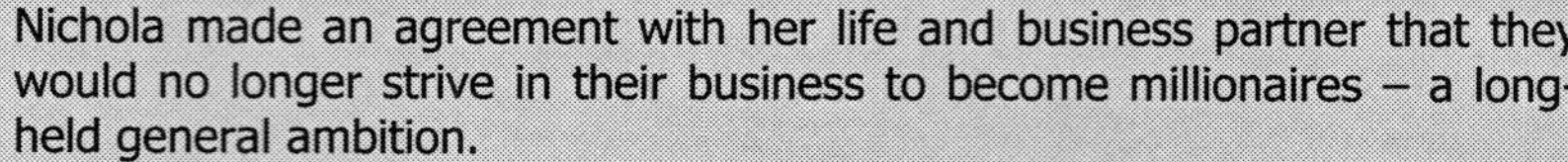

Nichola made an agreement with her life and business partner that they would no longer strive in their business to become millionaires – a long-held general ambition.

Although this was perhaps not such a difficult goal to achieve, the decision to abandon the goal actually had a major impact on their attitude and enjoyment at work.

They re-aligned what was and what was not important to them and adjusted their outputs to qualitative rather than quantitative measures, redefining their business model. They adjusted their client list, (choosing to work only with those people who they liked and who energised them), adjusted the kind of work they chose to accept (only doing those things that they enjoyed delivering and which provided outcomes that they could feel truly proud of) and they set a maximum number of nights in a year that they would each spend away from the family home on business.

By having a bigger 'Yes' (a clear picture of what we do want to achieve and what we are really committed to), it is much easier to come to terms with *not* doing certain things and to have the strength to say: 'No'.

For most people, the biggest factor that is preventing them from moving forward is actually themselves. Making progress is simply about making some choices about what to do and what not to do.

Have you noticed how you can always clear your desk or finish off outstanding tasks at home before you hit the deadline of going on holiday. How do you do that?

Once we accept that we cannot do everything, it is easier to make some proactive choices to do the things that we most need to do, to be successful.

Carl Lewis, 9 times Olympic gold medallist, expresses this well. He says:

"There are 3 keys to success.
First, work out what you want to achieve.
Second, work out the price associated with that achievement.
Third, pay that price.
Most people only get two out of three."

The hard part is not to find things to do, but to decide which are the *right* things to do.

High-quality, SMART goals

In order for goals to work they need to be high-quality goals. The principle of setting '**SMART**' goals is well established, where the goals are Specific, Measurable, Achievable, Realistic and Time-Bound. I have my own variation of this, and prefer to use the A for 'Agreed':

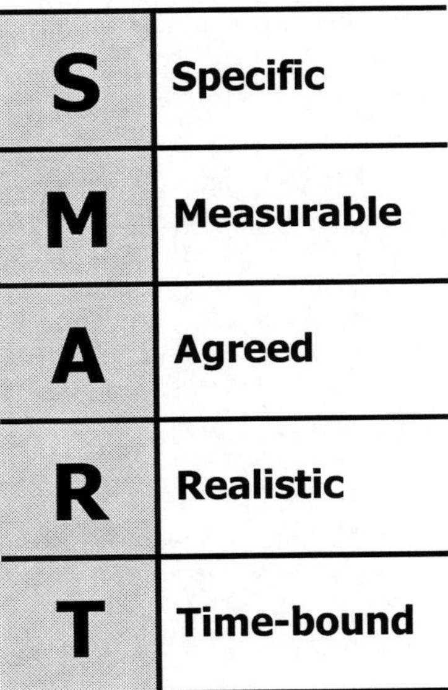

S	**Specific**
M	**Measurable**
A	**Agreed**
R	**Realistic**
T	**Time-bound**

Figure 15

Specific. Think back to the days when you were at school. Imagine going on a biology field trip and being given a square metre marked out with pegs and a piece of string in a field and being told to study the life forms that are held within it – you might be amazed how much there is to find. Of course, the biology teacher is pretty clever – rather than allowing everyone to work randomly, and perhaps superficially, across the whole field – they actually encourage people to put their 'stakes in the ground' and to fully engage with a specific piece of the whole.

Measurable. Businesses have goals and targets that are measurable – percentage increase of profitable sales year on year, staff turnover rates, target ROI and the like – and individuals have them too. Simply saying: "I want to lose weight" does not offer any measures for success. So beginning with a current weight and deciding on a target weight is a left-brain (logical) way of monitoring progress. A more right brained (creative) way might be to say something like: "I want to lose weight, so that I can wear my grey suit and feel really comfortable in it". Less quantifiable in figures, but very quantifiable for the individual – they will certainly know when they have achieved it and whether they feel good or not!

Agreed. Imagine a manager and their subordinate sitting down to define the business goals for the coming year. Four goals are driven by the manager and one is fought for and truly owned by the subordinate. If there is any conflict between these goals during the year in terms of time or resource allocation, which is the subordinate most likely to work on? Getting buy-in at the goal-setting process is fundamentally important because, unless they are micro-managed, it is the subordinate who will go away and do the work to progress the achievement of a goal on a day-to-day basis. It is inevitable that, consciously or unconsciously, they will have a priority order and for most people, the one that is highest in their values, the one that they are committed to, is likely to come first.

Realistic – and achievable. A well-set goal should be within our grasp and within our sphere of control. A track athlete might set a target to be World Champion. In their eyes this may be achievable, but even assuming they are physically able, success is also dependent on a number of outside factors – not least what other athletes do on any given day or in any given race. Much better that the athlete focus on achieving a personal best (which might also enable them to become the World Champion), but which is entirely within their own control. Setting this as a target means that in a race where a competitor does something extraordinary and wins, our athlete will maintain a sense of proportion – and focus on their own success. If they run second they can say: "I have achieved a personal best, run my best race ever", as opposed to saying "I didn't win the race".

Time-bound – well-set, high quality goals are always time-based. They have a clear starting time and a clear finishing time with milestones established along the way. Without this time orientation, it is easier to procrastinate and lose shape to the process, than it is to make progress.

In fact, I would go one stage further. Well-set, high quality goals should be **SMARTER** than the average goal:

S	**Specific**
M	**Measurable**
A	**Agreed**
R	**Realistic**
T	**Time-bound**
E	**Exciting**
R	**Recorded**

Figure 16

The first new letter is **E**, which stands for **Exciting**.

Exciting – when people have goals that they have really bought into, they are genuinely excited by them. They think about them, fantasise about achieving them – they become part of what they are and what they do. If a goal is exciting to an individual, then it is touching the very heart of what it is that motivates and inspires that person. If the goal turns them on, it becomes a beacon of their very being.

The second new letter is **R,** which stands for **Recorded**.

Recorded – well-set, high quality goals need to be referred to occasionally. Having them written down or recorded means that the goal owner can refer to them and begin the process of converting what otherwise might be an aspiration into an actuality. The process of converting a goal into a plan and then into what we actually do is key to results-oriented planning. If planning is taking place it must be done in conjunction with the goals. Having goals written down serves to remind us exactly what we are aspiring to and will help to measure the extent of progress, reassuring us that we are on the right track or spurring us on to greater activity.

The key to having well-set goals is to make them SMARTER. If an individual owns them, is stretched by them and believes that the goals are possible to achieve, then the goals are more likely to be motivational.

If a goal is motivational, then it is more likely to be worked on, which in turn makes it more likely that it will be achieved – helping to turn an ordinary performer into an excellent performer and a proven goal-misser into a proven goal-scorer.

Case Study 10:

Creating a 'proven goal scorer' – a fan's story

In the 2000-2001 season at Old Trafford, home of Manchester United, Jimmy Floyd Hasselbaink, playing in a Premiership match scored probably his best ever goal for Chelsea. I was high up in the North Stand with my son and three coach-loads of United supporters who had travelled together for the game.

The ball came to Jimmy Floyd outside of the United penalty area. He seemed to stop; he turned and looked at the crowd. My son and I looked at each other, and we both knew that he was going to score. I put my head in my hands, I looked at my son, he had his head in his hands, I looked at the three coach-loads of people who had travelled with us and they all had their head in their hands. Even the United goalkeeper had his head in his hands. Everybody, including Jimmy Floyd, knew that Jimmy Floyd would score. He was at the peak of his game, superbly confident, a proven goal scorer.

Within five minutes at the other end of the pitch, Nicky Butt received the ball on the edge of the 6 yard area. The defenders and the goalkeeper moved to one side to make it easier for him to shoot. Nicky turned and looked at the crowd. My son and I looked at each other. We both knew that he was going to miss. I put my head in my hands. I looked at my son and he had his head in his hands. I looked at the three coach-loads of people who had travelled with us, and they all had their head in their hands. Even Nicky Butt had his head in his hands. Everybody, including Nicky, knew that Nicky would miss. Lacking in goal-scoring confidence, he was a proven goal-misser.

Where Jimmy Floyd saw the goal, Nicky saw the goalkeeper!

Badly set goals can lead to lack of motivation and a sense of underachievement. It is important that managers help individuals to set stretch targets – but also to ensure that these targets are achievable. In this way, the performer can break into a positive cycle of motivation.

The Cycle of Motivation

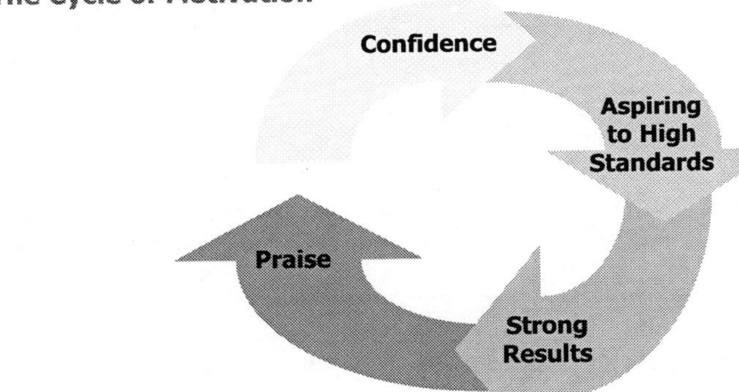

Figure 17

The Cycle of De-motivation

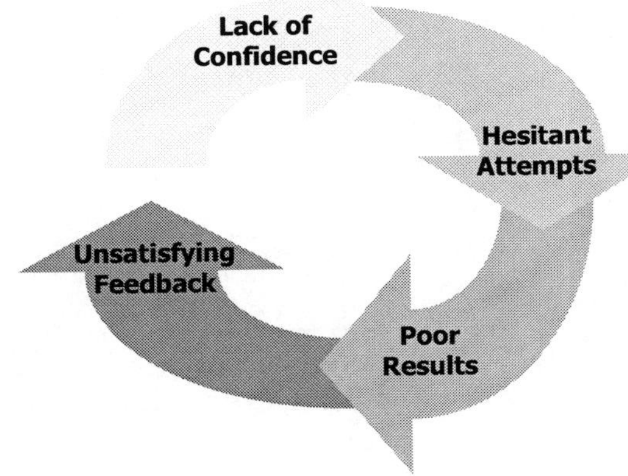

Figure 18

In business, is it a manager's responsibility to motivate his or her team, or is up to the whole team (including the manager) to create a culture and climate in which people can feel motivated?

Having well-set goals that people feel that they can achieve makes it much more likely that the working environment will feel positive and upbeat and that individuals will feel personally motivated.

What are the sources of your goals currently? (Think about both work and private life and the things that you do in the community.)

Are your goals high-quality and well set? Can you distinguish between dream, performance and process goals? Are yours SMARTER goals?

Are your goals manageable? Do they complement or conflict with each other?

Is there a good match between the goals that you are aspiring to, and how you currently spend your time? In other words, is working on your goals a part of your day-to-day, week-to-week plan?

In a few years time, how will you feel if you realise that there has been a mismatch between what you have spent your time on and what you have been aspiring to?

How can you make the link between goal and time allocation even tighter? Will you change your goals, so that they fall into line with what you do, or will you adjust what you do, in order to achieve your goals?

Why does goal-setting fail?

There are many reasons why the goal-setting process fails and people do not achieve their goals.

The most obvious failings are that people set unrealistic or conflicting goals, set goals which are not of a high enough quality and are certainly not **SMARTER,** or they do not see the process through.

Sometimes, goals are hard to quantify or are too ambitious and so become overwhelming. They may be set to a random timescale that has no connection with the realities of the world – or worse, are imposed, which means that they are not always seen as being realistic. They may not be exciting and therefore will not be motivational.

Another big failing is that too often goals are not written down, and are allowed to be vague. Without a clear definition of a goal, it is impossible to check whether the performer is 'on-line' or not. Writing goals down provides a means by which they can be compared one to another and allows a chronology or priority order of attack to be established.

It may also be that an individual has too many goals or that one goal conflicts with another. For example: "I want to have lots of holidays..." and "I want to progress in my job..." may not sit comfortably. Again, writing the goals down and achieving an overview will help to think this through.

Case Study 11:

Achieving clarity at Gdansk

In the early 1990's Bernie Schwarz was working in Poland at the Gdansk Ship Yard, the birthplace of 'Solidarity'. He was the British advisor to an American entrepreneur, who could see a fantastic opportunity to invest in an industry ripe for development.

Bernie found that most of the shipyard workers were either stuck in the Communist past... ("In the old days...", "When my father worked here...") or were living in the future, when somehow everything would be okay. His task was to give the people direction and help them through the difficult present. He began by sharing his vision with the workforce. He wanted to help them to build ships. Quality ships. Lots of them.

For their part, the workforce was clear about what they wanted – secure jobs and a lifestyle similar to that enjoyed in the West. They also knew that they had the profile to help the whole of the Polish economy to recover, ***if*** they got it right.

Bernie knew that it was going to be tough and that painful decisions would have to be made along the way, but it was apparent that history had provided them with opportunity as well as adversity and Bernie and his client decided that they should play to the shipyard's strengths – a large labour force used to receiving low wages.

They developed and published their vision: "We want to be recognised as a major World player in the production of low cost, high quality ships, within a year."

By refining this and quantifying how many tonnes of shipping would have to be produced and clarifying their timescales, they believed that they could achieve their vision, so long as certain dramatic steps were taken.

The entrepreneur now knew how long he would have to pour money into the shipyards for little or no return, and the workforce could begin to see a clear way forward. The labour force was restructured and retrained and individuals were helped to understand the part that they had to play in the rebirth.

Production targets of man-hours per tonne were established (in line with the rest of Europe) and 35 ships were to be produced at a fixed quality, by an agreed date.

For the first time people were clear about where they fitted in, what part they had to play and the impact that the things that they did 'today', 'this week' or 'this month' would have on them all achieving their dream.

Bernie's mantra or catchphrase at the time summed up his journey:

"The best way to predict your own future is to create it."

What Bernie was doing seemed to many people to be almost akin to rocket science. Luckily, rocket science is really very simple – it needs a combination of direction and momentum and, if either is missing, you cannot have a successful flight.

He provided clarity about the direction that the business needed to take, while the role of individual managers was to communicate that direction and ensure that their teams' energy was focused on the processes that they needed to go through to ensure they hit their performance targets. In other words, the managers' job was to ensure that their teams spent their time doing the newly-defined right things, right.

Goal setting – 3 years back and 3 years forward

Below is a goal setting exercise that you might like to try.

Stage 1: The left-hand column

On Figure 19, title the left hand column "This is me in xxxx" where xxxx is the year that you are currently in, **minus three years** (i.e. if the year now is 2007, write in 2004).

Now imagine that you are back in that year (2004) and that you have to make a presentation about yourself, thinking in the present tense even though you are going to be making notes about yourself as you were three years ago.

You will almost be running a DVD in your head of how you were 3 years ago – use it to brainstorm and list down bullet-point information about yourself down the left-hand column.

You might put things like: your name, age, job, salary, the vehicle you drive, relationships, where you live, who you live with, family, education, hobbies, interests, clubs, societies, holidays, community, social activity and so on...

Use your own headings and let your mind run free – the more information you put in, the better the result.

Stage 2: The right-hand column

Title the right-hand column "This is me in xxxx" where xxxx is the year that you are currently in **plus three years** (i.e. if the year now is 2007, write in 2010).

Again, think about yourself in the present tense; refer to the left-hand column and ask yourself the question: "If that is where I was six years ago, where am I today?"

You can refer to the entries on the left-hand side to help you capture more information on the right. Begin to write your new state down in the right-hand column. This will offer some anchor points to help you to think about where you will be in three years time.

As you go through this process you will realise that there are many other things not referred to at all in the left-hand column which you would like to put in the right hand column – put them in. Again, the more the better.

If you find it impractical to go 3 years back and 3 years forward, try 2 and 2 or 1 and 1 – but always use a matching time differential from the present.

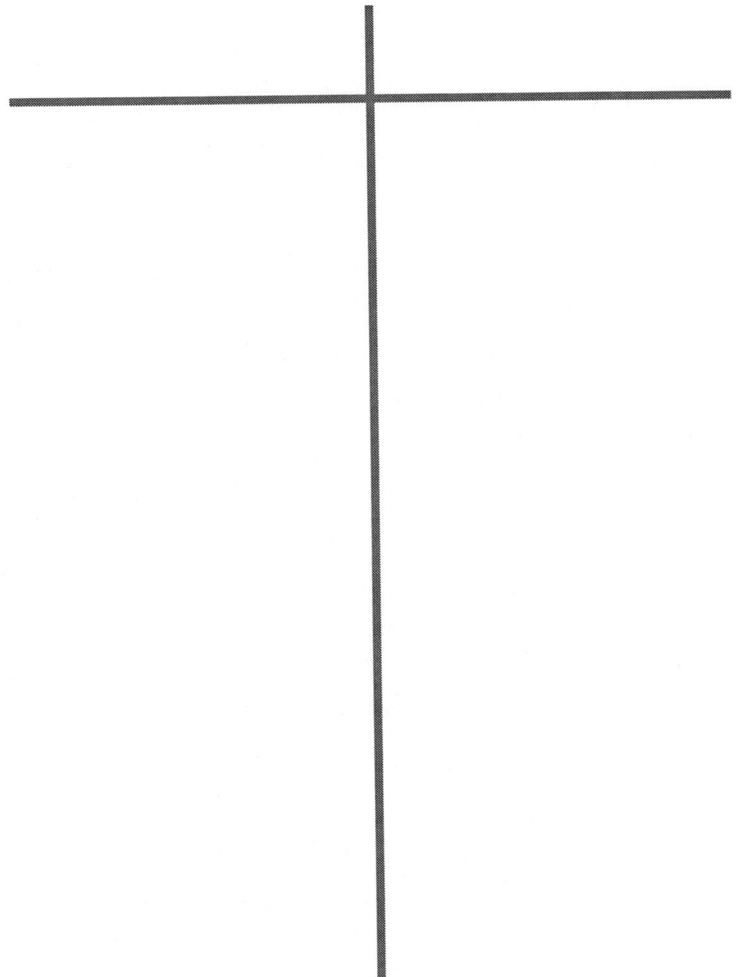

Figure 19

What did you notice as you were going through the process?

____

____

____

Looking back 3 years there may be some things that you reflect on which make you unhappy. You cannot change the things that have already happened.

People are different. Some are able to look back over the last 3 years and say:

"My goodness, everything has changed."

Others might look back and say:

"Nothing has changed."

There is of course no right or wrong – but it might be useful to notice the extent to which you proactively planned what happened to you over the last 3 years and to what extent it just happened!

Would you like to have a greater say in what happens in the next 3 years? If so, what? In which areas of your life?

____

____

____

If there is no dramatic difference in your two lists, be aware that sometimes we have to work very hard just to stay still.

Understanding the lists

There is a good chance that the headings that you wrote down in the right hand column are performance goals. If these are clustered together and given a group heading, such as "This is me being happy...", or "This is me being successful", then you will have identified your dream goal, (the compelling reason for you doing what you do), for the next three years.

The key now is to prioritise these performance goals and identify a logical order for action. As you begin to plan what you need to do, you are in fact identifying your process goals. Remember to make sure that all of your goals are SMARTER.

Take time to analyse and understand your process goals:

- ❑ Are some short-term, while others are longer-term?
- ❑ Do any conflict or contradict each other?
- ❑ Is achieving some dependant on having achieved others first?
- ❑ Are your performance goals in line with the goals of the other people and organisations in your life?

Once you have identified what you need to do, it is imperative that these 'right things' find some space in your diary!

The 3 years back and 3 years forward exercise was based around private life. You can of course use exactly the same method to establish your business goals.

Work through the process again and use the Goal Recording Pro-forma which you will find in Appendix 1 to pull together your ideas.

Recording and checking goals

Goal Recording Pro-forma

In the examples below, (see Figures 20 and 21) we have shown the way that one individual recorded their dream, performance and process goals. Figure 20 is based on goals linked to aspects of working life.

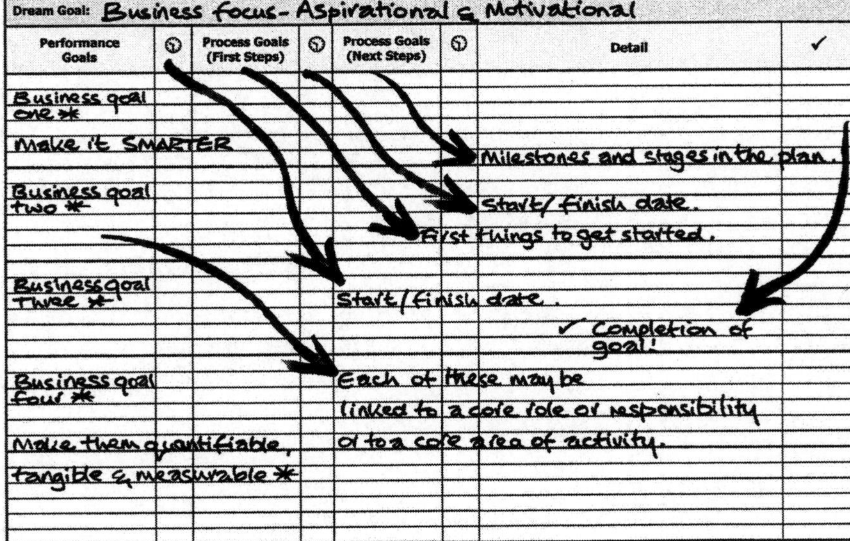

Figure 20

Figure 21 is linked to areas of private life.

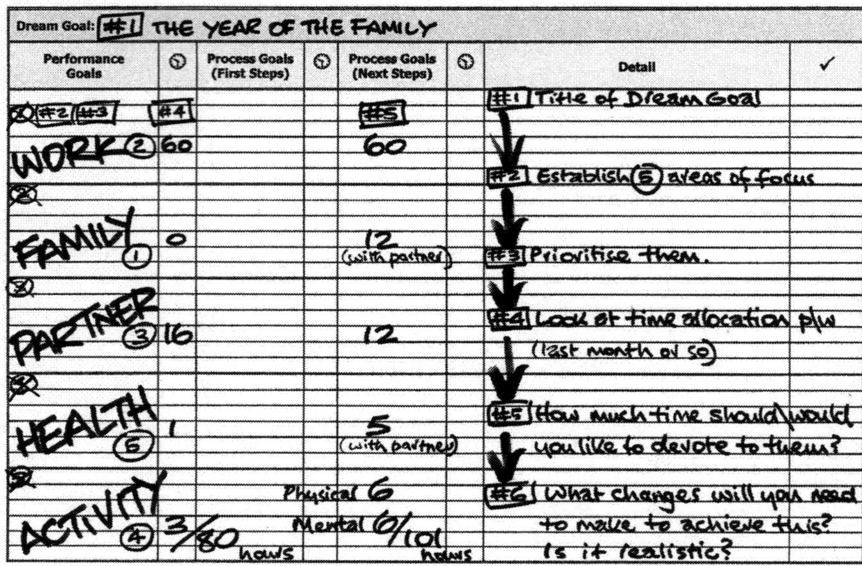

Dream Goal: #1 THE YEAR OF THE FAMILY

Performance Goals	⏱	Process Goals (First Steps)	⏱	Process Goals (Next Steps)	⏱	Detail	✓
#2 #3	#4			#5		#1 Title of Dream Goal	
WORK ②	60			60			
						#2 Establish ⑤ areas of focus	
FAMILY ①	0			12 (with partner)		#3 Prioritise them.	
PARTNER ③	16			12		#4 Look at time allocation p/w (last month or so)	
HEALTH ⑤	1			5 (with partner)		#5 How much time should/would you like to devote to them?	
ACTIVITY ④	3/80 hours	Physical		6		#6 What changes will you need to make to achieve this?	
		Mental		6/101 hours		Is it realistic?	

Figure 21

It will take some time, thought and discussion with other interested parties to complete the Goal Recording Pro-forma fully. Having thought it through, keep checking that the process goals are appearing in your plans and in your diary.

- ❑ Remind yourself of your goals as part of your monthly planning.
- ❑ Check your progress.
- ❑ Review your goals and reset them if they are no longer as relevant as they once were.

Setting and recording SMARTER goals is a necessary precursor of prioritisation and effective time management.

There are many other methods you can use for goal-setting and visualisation.

Act as if!

This is rather like method acting, where in order to play the part, the actor 'becomes' the part. To use this method, you decide what it is you want to do, what behaviours you want to change or who you want to be, and you begin to live the life.

So, if you want to be an inventor, a song-writer, an author, a teacher, or a restaurateur, one route into it is to begin to behave as if you are one – to spend your time doing whatever it is that defines this role and (here's the important bit) not doing the sorts of things you were doing previously, which helped to define you as something else.

The thinking behind this might be: how can you invent, if you do not take time to be inquisitive, to make connections and to explore alternatives? How will you ever write a song without engaging with poetry and music or connecting with your inspiration? How can you be a teacher, unless you understand what and who you want to teach?

A person may have wanted to be an author for years, but it will never happen until they begin to 'think, believe and do' like an author does. They need to find their subject, do their research and begin the process of pouring out whatever it is they want to say.

"If you want to find new territory, you may have to leave the shade of the family tree."

Proverb of the Masai Tribe

Focus on it, dream it, plan it, do it!

If you want something badly enough – if something is really important to you – then you will probably spend time thinking about it. If the thinking is positive, it will become a glowing visualisation of success and as soon as the visualisation is rooted in reality, it will flip from fantasy to fact.

This transfer is well documented and is particularly well explained by John Nabers, the Olympic 100m Backstroke Gold Medallist in 1976, who talks about the importance of having goals, breaking them down into tasks and actually spending time implementing the plan.

Case Study 12:

From dream to goal

In 1972, Mark Spitz won seven gold medals, breaking seven world records. I was at home watching him on my living room floor and I said to myself at the time, "Wouldn't it be nice to be able to win a gold medal, to be able to be a world champion in Olympic competition?" So right then I was dreaming of being an Olympic champion, and almost immediately the dream became a goal. That dream to goal transition is the biggest thing I learned prior to Olympic competition – how important it is to set a goal. Certainly, motivation is important. A lot of kids have motivation, "Gee, I'd love to be great..."

My personal best in the 100m backstroke was 59.5. Roland Matthes winning the same event for the second consecutive Olympics (1972) went 56.3. I extrapolated his three Olympic performances and I figured in 1976, 55.5 would be the order of the day. That's what I figured I'd have to do. So I'm four seconds off the shortest backstroke event on the Olympic programme. It's the equivalent of dropping four seconds in the 440-yard dash.

It's a substantial chunk. But because it's a goal now I can decisively figure out how I can attack that. I have four years to do it in. I'm watching TV in 1972. I've got four years to train. So it's only one second a year. That's still a substantial chunk. Swimmers train ten or eleven months a year so it's about a tenth of a second a month, giving time off for missed workouts. And you figure we train six days a week so it's only about 1/300th of a second a day. We train from six to eight in the morning and four to six at night so it's really only about 1/1200th of a second every hour. Do you know how short a 1200th of a second is? Look at my hand and blink when I snap, would you, please? OK, from the time your eyelids started to close to the time they touched 5/1200th of a second elapsed. For me to stand on a pool deck and say, "During the next 60 minutes I'm going to improve that much," that's a believable dream. I can believe in myself. I can't believe that I'm going to drop four seconds by the next Olympics, but I can believe I can get that much faster. Couldn't you? Sure. So all of a sudden, I'm moving.

What John Nabers is describing here is a life-defining moment. An occasion when with a blinding flash, he discovered a deep and compelling sense of purpose, which shaped his thinking and his very being for the next several years. In these few paragraphs, he offers a clear guide of the dream-to-goal, goal-to-plan, plan-to-implementation process and he gives a fantastic example of using the Salami Technique (see page 100).

The first 100 days

I am particularly struck by the concept of 'the first 100 days'. On his inauguration as President of the United States of America, Franklin D Roosevelt set himself a target of his first 100 days in office to begin to make a difference. He asked not to be judged until he had completed those 100 days.

I have found it useful when applying for a job, or when taking on a new responsibility or team to set myself the task of thinking through, and then presenting to my sponsors, where I wanted to be after 100 days.

This works particularly well, partly because 100 days is just over three months; it's long enough to engage, to think, to plan and to lay down the threads for implementation. It is a manageable time to think through and, when positioned as part of a long-term strategy, is a sensible point at which, on the one hand to aim for tangible successes, and on the other to pause and think through the journey and successes so far.

Have a plan and start!

"If not now, then when? If not you, then who?"

Sergey Bubka's Coach, Vitaly Petro

Sergey Bubka was 6 times consecutive IAAF World Pole Vault Champion and won a Gold Medal at the Seoul Olympics.

Your 80th birthday party

Congratulations! It's your 80th Birthday and your family are going to celebrate. Pause. Imagine the scene right now.

What is it like? Who is there? What are the expressions on their faces? What are you like? What is your mood? How do you feel in the moment?

Did you imagine you were lying in a hospital bed with one or two people looking glum and forcing some conversation because – hey, you have made it to 80!

Or, did you imagine a rather more uplifting scene? Perhaps a party?

In my mind's eye, I imagine myself arriving at a big family house in the country. It's a sunny day – it must be summer (even though my birthday is in November). I have been collected for the party by one of my grandchildren who is tall and healthy. Strangely, so am I. Younger children and grandchildren are playing in the garden. Some rush up to me. Others wave while they continue to play cricket. When the ball comes to me I have no problem running up to the wicket and bowling a perfect spin ball… you get the idea.

At 80, I am going to be fit and healthy living in an ideal world where the sun always shines – these must be the good old days of the future!

In true goal-setting style, maybe I should ask myself the question: "If that is where I want to be in 40 years time, what am I doing about it today? Do I look after my health? Do I nurture my relationships? Am I, or all of the people who matter to me, going to want or be able to take part in this dream?"

Once I get inside the door and we have a big dinner, it's time for the speeches. Everyone wants to say something. It makes me think if my Mum or Dad were there, what would I want them to say about me? And as I look around, I wonder what my wife will say after 60 plus years of marriage. My kids, my best friend... Again, you get the picture.

I know just the sorts of things I would like them to say – some of the words I use to describe myself and my character when I fill in applications for a job – but what would they really be able to say? That I was kind? Loyal? A real family man? Who knows? it rather depends on how I spend my time between now and then.

With this visualisation I have begun to define the destination that I want to arrive at in some 40 years time. All I have to do now is spend time on the right journey!

Learning from Alice!

Alice is walking through the woods and the path splits in two. The Cheshire cat is sitting in the tree.

Alice says: "Will you tell me, please, which way ought I to go?"

"That depends a good deal on where you want to get to," said the Cat.

"I don't much care where," said Alice.

"Then it doesn't matter which way you go," said the Cat.

"... so long as I get somewhere," Alice added as an explanation.

"Oh, you are sure to do that," said the Cat, "if only you walk long enough."

Sometimes people are so busy getting where they are going that it is only when they pause that they realise that where they are is not quite where they wanted to end up.

As they look back, they may wonder why they spent so much time and energy working hard to get to the wrong place!

Case Study 13:

Living other people's dreams

I once ran a Time Management workshop that was attended by an internationally famous sportsman. He was captain of his national team, successful in business and had a loving family. Along with everyone else in the room, I was rather in awe of him.

He spoke to me in the first coffee break, telling me that he was really in need of some help with his time management. I asked him what he did.

He said:

"You may know, (I did!), I'm captain of my national side. I've just come back off tour and am quite involved in marketing the World Cup as my federation is the host this year. I play for my club, where I am captain, but I have to work hard to keep my place in the team. I coach the Colts, because I think it's important to give something back to the sport, and I am president of the club, which is a great honour, and I have to attend quite a few dinners and events. I have a career and my boss tells me that if I want to build my career, I need to be doing some proactive things to set me apart from my colleagues, possibly over and above the standard 39 hours a week. I have a family and they are very important to me."

I asked him to put those things in order of time allocation and he said:

"Oh, that's easy – first it's my club, second is my country, third is my job, and fourth is my family".

I knew that we needed to get started with the training course, so I said:

"OK, just have a think through for when we next speak – if you had to prioritise, what would be the order of priority for you currently in those four areas?" and again he said:

"That's easy too – obviously my family is the most important thing in my life!"

We both just looked at each other and then he turned and walked out of the room.

I did not see him again for the rest of the two-day workshop, but he called me up the day after and said he thought he needed some help.

The word in the press was that he was going through some sort of breakdown – he resigned as national captain, he scaled down his commitment to the non-playing side of his club and he got focused on what was really important to him.

He told me afterwards that previously, wherever he went people told him how successful he was, but he had suddenly realised that he was only successful by other people's standards and that in fact he was living other people's dreams. He suddenly understood that he was in danger of being seen as a failure by the people he cared about most – his family and most importantly for his self-esteem, himself.

Setting goals with a partner

Step 1: Sit down with your partner and each list three things that you want for the other person in the coming year. Be aware: you may find each others ideas to be somewhere on a continuum between generous and outlandish – but try not to worry about that at the creative stage.

Step 2: Each list three things that you want for yourself in the coming year.

Step 3: Share all of your ideas.

You will very quickly get a picture of what you both want (and what you both thought that the other person wanted) and where the touch points actually are.

This clarity can lead to a focused discussion of the implications of what you are both aspiring to, for yourselves as individuals and for the two of you as a partnership – it will certainly mean that the aspiration-to-goal journey is likely to be more realistic.

This sharing of ideas will also provide you with the opportunity to clarify, and begin to prioritise in the short, medium and long term.

Setting goals with a family

You can develop the exercise outlined above with a wider family group – perhaps first taking the precaution of making it clear that this is a discussion, not a contract!

In a mature family environment, this will lead to a conversation about values, alignment and the implications of taking one course of action above the possibility of being able to follow another.

Conversations will range through fairness, equality, cost and apparent benefit – and so may not be comfortable for all family groups to attempt!

This is a great exercise to help younger family members begin to understand opportunity cost, comparative values of activity, the need for give-and-take, and perhaps even that that machine in the wall at the Bank has to have money put in, before it can be taken out!

So, why bother to have goals?

The goal-setting process enables us to think and prioritise, as a result of which we are more likely to be able to set off on, and have the confidence to stick to, the right track.

Goal-setting can be a long and iterative process, but it is one where the pain is definitely worth the gain, and where the benefits of getting things right in the medium and long term greatly outweigh any costs incurred through time investment in the short term.

"If you don't know where you are going, any path will take you there."

Chapter 4

Managing Tasks and Prioritisation

- Avoiding a 'butterfly day'
- Efficient v Effective
- The Daily Task Tracker
- Further applications (1)
- The 4 D's
- Pareto's principle
- Costing your time and calculating your success
- Further applications (2)
- Priority v Pay-off Matrix
- The Urgent and Important Matrix
- Prioritising the boxes
- Achieving major tasks
- Eating salami
- Case Study 14
- Action Planning Pro-forma
- Getting into Box 1... and out again!

For most people, when they have more to do than can be comfortably fitted in to the confines of a day, they deal with the immediate, the urgent, the things that rush up and bite them on the leg ... and on these sorts of days the things that do not get done are things like taking lunch, going home on time, taking time to think or to plan, long-term tasks or projects. In other words, reactive, short-term, busy things stay in the day and get done. Longer-term, proactive, developmental things are left for another day. Not much of a way to build a business or a career for that matter!

This is a description of a 'butterfly day', a day where the butterfly alights on one thing momentarily before it's attention is pulled away to another distraction and then to another and then another... and so on. There is no shape, no structure and busyness quickly replaces effectiveness.

Avoiding a 'butterfly day'

The best way to avoid a butterfly day, is to have focus and to get in control early.

One method that works for many people is to make sure that they have a clear plan in place before they can get deflected. Part of this is to finalise plans (as far as possible) for each day, **before they get to it**.

To achieve this, at the end of each day take time out to review what has and has not been done. Enjoy your successes and identify those things that need to be carried forward into the next day's plans.

Having planned a set of good intentions, you can take off the 'working head' and go home. You have thought through your plans for tomorrow – so forget about them.

Arriving at work the next day, there will no doubt be a million-and-one things that have to be done, but if you have a plan you can simply put it beside these new 'alternatives' and decide which you are actually going to do and which you are not going to allow to deflect you.

Prioritisation is impossible if the day has not been planned in advance. Without a plan to set new opportunities beside, well-judged decisions cannot be made and, as the opportunity cost of choosing one thing above another is not apparent, there is a tendency to go for the quick, the easy, the exciting and to focus on quantity rather than quality.

People who arrive at work without a plan often get deflected, but do not realise it until the end of the day when they look back and recognise they have been busy, but feel that they have achieved nothing.

Efficient v Effective

It is important not to confuse being efficient with being effective. At best, efficiency is about doing things right, while effectiveness is about doing the right things, right.

There used to be a programme on British television called 'The Crystal Maze'. At the end of the show, contestants would go into an air-tight room, filled with bank note sized pieces of silver foil, with a few gold foil pieces mixed in. They were instructed to collect high value gold foil, while any lower value silver that they collected would count against them. An air machine blew the foil around the room and the contestants tried to collect the highest total value of foil notes that they could in the time available.

Over a number of episodes, it was clear that different contestants would follow different strategies – some focused on collecting volume, grabbing everything (including lots of silver), whilst others focused on just collecting fewer of the high value gold foil. In many ways, this demonstrates the efficient verses effective dilemma. The efficient person might reason that they could save energy and collect a greater volume of gold by focusing on picking up as many foil notes as possible – and hoping that their gold total would outweigh the silver. The effective people however, tended to adopt a different strategy, setting their goal as being to find and capture the high value gold foil only, disregarding the silver – picking up less, but ensuring greater value.

The Daily Task Tracker

We have identified that good time and task management is not about being busy; it is about doing the right things, right. The Daily Task Tracker illustrated in Figure 22 below is a development of what John Adair would call a Time Log (see Appendix 2 for a full-sized version). It is intended to be used as a tool for recording what you actually do, so that you can learn some lessons and ensure that you are focusing on the right things – dealing with the gold foil and ignoring the silver!

1	2	3	4	5	6
1A-3C	Box 1-4	Start Time	Task Description	Time Taken	Ideas for Smartening up Time & Task Management

Figure 22

In order to gather data, focus initially on columns three, four and five. You should attempt to keep fairly good records for two or three days, after which you will have a good sense of how you are spending your time.

As soon as you arrive at work, log your start time. Make a note of the task you are doing. I tend to use icons or abbreviations for this.

Telephone

Meeting

Client Visit

Training

Coffee Break

1:1 Meeting

Working from Home

Working from Office / On-site

Travel

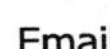

Email

Snail Mail

Report / Proposal Writing

Administration

Recovery time

When you finish, record how long you spent on the activity.

At the end of your recording period, you will have some excellent information about how you really spend your time in the work place. Put aside 15-20 minutes at the end of the week to review columns 3, 4 and 5. What strikes you? You may be surprised by the gaps and time that is lost chatting, or moving from place to place.

Examples of the sorts of things to look out for:

- You might notice that there are times in the day where it is very busy or noisy in your work environment and it is hard to concentrate.

  Could you plan to do the tasks that demand most concentration at a different time of day? Could you create a quiet time or space for yourself to work in?

- You may notice that you have a colleague who interrupts you 17 times (count them!) in one day, each time asking only one thing.

  Could you encourage this colleague to save all of their points for a specific meeting, once a day or every other day, where you discuss 17 things? It is quite likely that having saved up all of their agenda for one hit, many items will not seem as important as they did when they were being asked spontaneously. Having a planned meeting may also give you an opportunity to educate and coach your colleague, to prevent them from asking the same kinds of question or for the same information over and over again – as well as allowing you to introduce subjects from your own agenda.

- ❑ You may recognise there are times of day when you are particularly high or low in energy.

  Can you spot a pattern? What (who) is it that energises you? What (who) is it that de-energises you? How can you seek out more of the energisers and less of the de-energisers? Could you match appropriate tasks to your energy level, doing simple, repetitive tasks when you are low in energy and dealing with the more complex, demanding tasks when you are high in energy?

Using the Daily Task Tracker, you may spot lots of things, but because this data is peculiar and particular to you, you will need to draw your own conclusions and create your own action plan for change.

You may also be interested to notice the relative return you get from some activities compared to others. Is it worth focusing on doing more of these high return activities?

As a result of this exercise, you will definitely be in a position to identify more clearly what is and what is not working, from which point you can begin to come up with some ideas as to how to save time and operate more effectively in the future. Use column 6 to record ways to do the things that you have done faster, better, or at a lower cost in future. Look for practical ideas and add these to the spreadsheet of ideas on page 17.

Keep records for at least three days, although a full week would be better, if you can manage it.

No doubt as you read this there is a little voice in your head screaming out: "I am too busy to do this", but without some good quality data, it is impossible to learn the lessons from your own performance or to plan to implement the changes that will enable you to raise your game.

Further applications (1)

So far, we have used the Daily Task Tracker to record what is done and then investigate ways to do it faster, or better, or to a lower cost. But what if some of the things being done are actually the wrong things?

It is not hard to find tasks to do; the hard thing is to decide what tasks **not to do** and either drop them, delay them or delegate them to other people.

Go through your completed Daily Task Tracker Pro-forma, imagining that for some reason (poor health, covering for a colleague, a new job opportunity) you only have 50% of the time that you would normally give to your job available for you to use.

The 4 D's

Take a different coloured highlighter pen for each of the 4 D's and mark on the Daily Task Tracker which task fits with which D:

- ❑ **Do it!** – If you have less time to do your job, which would be the tasks that **you would still have to do?** What are the key 20% of tasks for you?

- ❑ **Drop it!** – If you have less time to do your job, which would be the tasks that **you could stop doing?** These might well be things that you enjoy, that you are good at, or that you have always done – but which may not be key.

- ❑ **Delay it!** – If you have less time to do your job, which would be the tasks that you do which **only serve to keep you busy** and prevent you from doing the things that you really need to do?

- ❑ **Delegate it!** – If you have less time to do your job, which are the **tasks that other people could do adequately well**, if only you gave them the time, the space, the support and the encouragement?

Do you really need to wait for an outside influence (poor health, covering for a colleague etc) to help you progress the effectiveness of your task management?

When trying to decide whether to Do it, Drop it, Delay it or Delegate it, useful questions to ask yourself could be:

- ❑ What is the opportunity cost of my doing this task?
  (i.e. If I do this, what else is it preventing me from doing?)
- ❑ What is the financial cost of this? – (see Figure 24)
  (i.e. is it worth the current level of investment of my / our time?)
- ❑ Will doing this task help me to achieve my goals?
- ❑ Am I the best person to do this job anyway?
- ❑ Am I directing my subordinates to the highest priority tasks? (Do I know what they are?)

The case for proactivity – where to record the 4 D's

- ❑ Tasks to Do should be proactively planned into some kind of Daily Plan (page 49).
- ❑ Tasks to Delay should be stored on a Gap-filler List Pro-forma (page 178).
- ❑ Tasks to be Delegated should be delegated and recorded on a Delegated Tasks Pro-forma (page 123).
- ❑ Tasks to Drop (dump or delete) can go into the bin, ***today.***

Look back at your Daily Task Tracker. What % of your time do you spend on each type of activity?

Type of Activity	Time Spent	% of total time	Type of Activity	Time Spent	% of total time

Figure 23

How does this data compare with what you expected? Where have you got opportunities to make adjustments in your choice of tasks?

____

____

____

If you are not going to do something, why not save both time and stress – decide not to do it now!

Pareto's principle

In 1906, the Italian economist Vilfredo Pareto presented a mathematical formula to describe the unequal distribution of wealth in Italy. He observed that twenty percent of the population owned eighty percent of the wealth, which meant that eighty percent of the population shared the remaining twenty percent. His 80/20 rule, thereafter known as Pareto's Principle, was popularised in the 1940s, when Joseph Juran applied it to his own area of expertise – quality management.

In recent times, the 80/20 rule has become well known to sales people, who often work with a ratio that says that 80% of their business comes from 20% of their customers, which means that 20% of their business comes from the remaining 80%. This ratio also holds true to a great extent in time management, where value can be taken from an individual finding the key 20% of tasks which allow them to deliver the 80% of their results, which they should focus on. Similarly, finding the 80% of tasks which deliver only 20% of results, gives them the opportunity to do something proactive about these low return tasks and to find a way to stop doing them!

Having used the Daily Task Tracker, think about other things that you spend your time on in your job, but which did not fall into the period where you kept records. These may include:

- ❑ Things that happen on an irregular or cyclical basis.
- ❑ Reactive or proactive things.
- ❑ Things that are company specific or externally focused.
- ❑ Things that you do by yourself or as part of a team.

For all of the tasks that you do, ask yourself:

- ❑ Does this work have to be done at all? Do I have to do it? If so, does it have to be done now?
- ❑ What would happen if no-one did it?
- ❑ How does it relate to my core areas of activity and to my own objectives?
- ❑ If I do this work, what will I be unable to do?

Which of the tasks on the Daily Task Tracker bring you the most benefit for the least cost, in terms of time or effort?

____

____

____

Which of these tasks must you **Do**?

Which of the other tasks can you **Drop**?

Which of the other tasks can you **Delay**?

Which of the other tasks can you **Delegate**?

Costing your time and calculating your success

Further impetus may be given to the thinking process when the cost to the business of each individual's time input is also factored in.

Using Figure 24 may help you to realise that there are some tasks that you are drawn into, which are no longer appropriate for you to do and given your £$€ cost to the company, you should really find a way to move on, to focus instead on the important and high value things.

Calculate how much **you** cost your business per hour. You might also find it useful to calculate the hourly rate for each member of your team.

Annual Salary	**£$€**
Add in the value of any perks (discounts, bonuses and commissions payable)	**£$€**
+ Employers pension/National Insurance contributions	**£$€**
+ 100% Allowance for Overheads/Infrastructure	**£$€**
Your Total Cost to the Company	**£$€ per annum**
÷ 220 (the average number of working days)	**£$€ per day**
÷ the average number of hours you work each day	**£$€ per hour**

Figure 24

It is very important to keep a record of how much time you have saved by Dropping, Delaying or Delegating tasks. How you spend the time that you generate is up to you – some people use it to invest in planning and preparation, others to develop their team. Some even use it to take breaks or to go home on time!

The choice is yours, but enjoy the pleasure and reduction in stress that you get from feeling in control and driving your task management.

Calculate your success in Figure 25, over the page.

Task	Action: Dropped / Delayed / Delegated	Time Saved	£ $ € Saved

Figure 25

Is there any learning that you can take from this to share with your wider team or with other colleagues?

____

____

____

Further applications (2)

When justifying why we have chosen to do one task ahead of another, we often use some common buzz-words:

I have to do this because...

- ❑ ...it is a priority.
- ❑ ...it has a high pay-off.
- ❑ ...it is urgent.
- ❑ ...it is important.

Priority v Pay-off Matrix

Figure 26 below is a quick model, much beloved of the Institute of Directors, which may help you to decide which tasks should really gain your attention.

For each task simply ask yourself:

"Where does this task fit in on the priority and pay-off axis?"

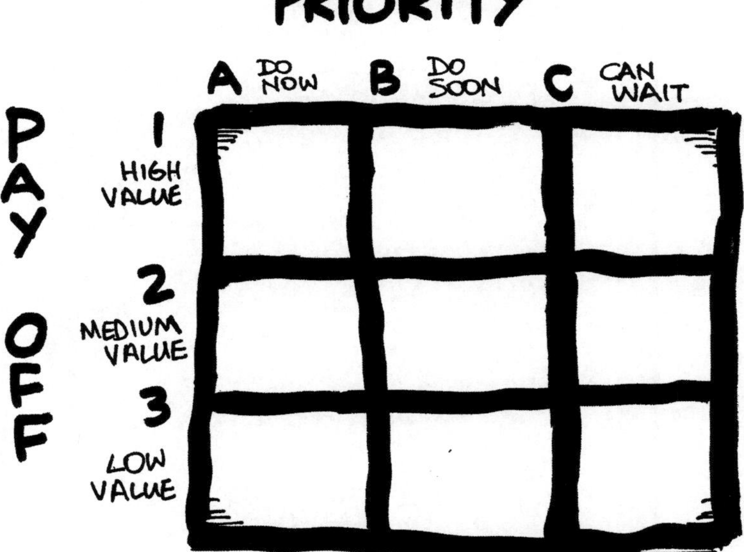

Figure 26

... and the good advice is, if you do not have time for everything, focus on your 1A, 1B and 1C entries!

Many people have particular trouble getting around to doing 1C tasks. They are **Important but Not Urgent** and do not get done because there is a tendency to prioritise based on 'urgency', regardless off 'pay-off'.

However, be aware that what lives in this box are often the proactive, developmental or maintenance things – which, if we do not do them, eventually come back to bite us! We will address this later in the chapter.

If you must focus on the trivial, do low pay-off tasks (3A, 3B and 3C), as quickly as possible and to the minimum quality required. If possible, do not do them at all.

Refer back to the Daily Task Trackers that you have completed. Scan through the tasks that you have done and using column 1 (which we have not used until now), mark off where they fit in on the priority matrix 1A – 3C scale. This may give you more confidence to ruthlessly apply the 4 D's!

Why not use the Priority / Pay-Off Matrix to help you to identify your most high-value tasks and to prioritise them as you receive them.

If you do not have time for everything it would be smart to stay in Row 1 as much as possible.

Do not be afraid to say "NO!" to the other tasks. It is OK to say "NO!" when:

- ❑ the request is unreasonable.
- ❑ the task has low priority to you.
- ❑ the task need not be done by you at all.

Remember, it is easier to say "NO!" when you have a bigger "YES!"

The Urgent and Important Matrix

People deal with and prioritise diverse tasks differently.

However, everything that we work on can be plotted somewhere on the Urgent and Important Matrix, first developed by Alan Lakein (see Figure 27).

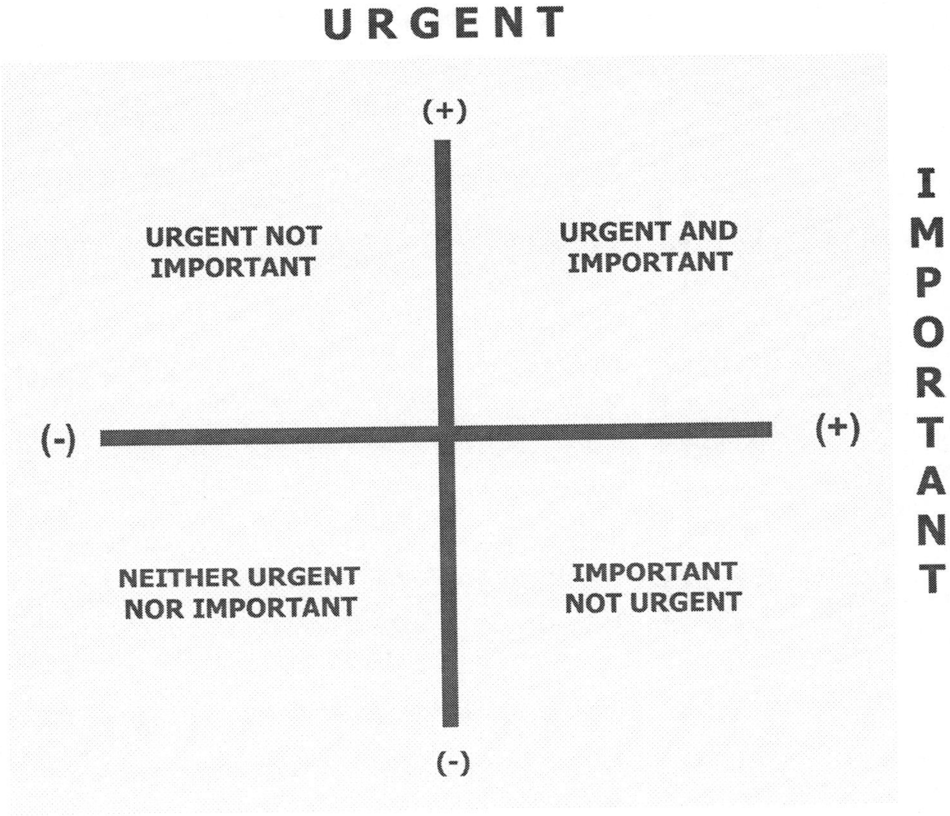

URGENT

(+)

URGENT NOT IMPORTANT

URGENT AND IMPORTANT

(-) (+)

I M P O R T A N T

NEITHER URGENT NOR IMPORTANT

IMPORTANT NOT URGENT

(-)

Figure 27

Let's visit each of the boxes in turn and begin with the top right hand box, **Urgent and Important**.

If yours is a fast-moving and vibrant business, you will probably recognise that in your job you are engaged in a lot of tasks and activities that are both urgent and important.

There is no doubt that you will be expected to deal with things that 'matter' and that need to be completed in the short term.

Make your own list of your **Urgent and Important** tasks below.

How would it feel if you 'lived' in this box permanently? How would you feel about yourself and the work that you do?

Now move to the top left hand box, **Urgent not Important**.

Do you ever find yourself having to deal with things which are clearly urgent, but of questionable importance to you? Often these tasks and activities will be delivered to you by other people – they are important to them and they are under time pressure, which they are now sharing with you! Many of us will find ourselves being pushed towards this box by our boss, our colleagues and our customers – all of whom, whether through lack of awareness, bad planning or disorganisation, deliver us with a crisis!

In the real world, we probably have no option but to 'pick up the baton' and run with it. We work hard and we come through for these people – and what message does this send out? "Don't bother to plan, I don't have priorities of my own, I am just waiting here to respond to you at a moment's notice. If I have to work late, that's fine with me".

Some managers often put their colleagues into this box, just through poor planning. By not planning and consequently delivering colleagues with a crisis that might have been avoided, they pull those colleagues away from their own priorities, tasks and objectives, which they have worked hard to fit into their day. These are good people and their boss relies on them to deliver – until the day comes when they decide that they are not prepared to be taken for granted any longer.

We cannot ignore those tasks or activities that come into the top left box – of course they have to be done. But we should let the people who put us into the box know that they are delivering us with a problem or a challenge and that it would be much easier for us if, in future, they would plan things differently.

Make your own list of **Urgent not Important** tasks below.

____

____

____

How would it feel if you 'lived' in this box permanently? How would you feel about yourself and the work that you do?

____

____

____

What about the bottom left hand box, **Neither Urgent nor Important**?

Do you ever notice other people doing things in this box? (I would not dream of asking whether you spend any time here!) It is much easier to spot other people. What sort of tasks live in this box?

Make your own list of **Neither Urgent nor Important** tasks below.

____

____

____

How would it feel if you 'lived' in this box permanently? How would you feel about yourself and the work that you do?

____

____

____

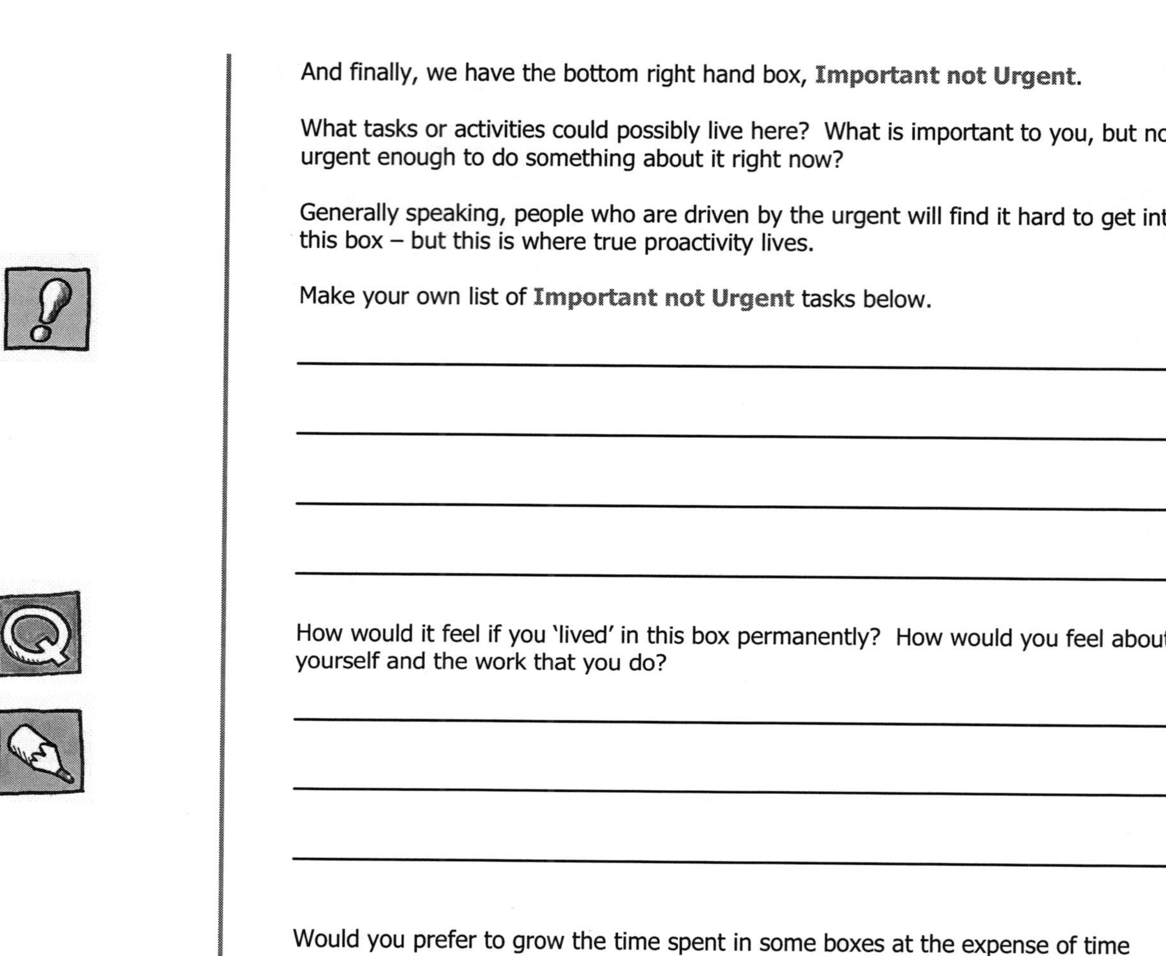

And finally, we have the bottom right hand box, **Important not Urgent**.

What tasks or activities could possibly live here? What is important to you, but not urgent enough to do something about it right now?

Generally speaking, people who are driven by the urgent will find it hard to get into this box – but this is where true proactivity lives.

Make your own list of **Important not Urgent** tasks below.

How would it feel if you 'lived' in this box permanently? How would you feel about yourself and the work that you do?

Would you prefer to grow the time spent in some boxes at the expense of time spent in others? If so, visualising yourself in a coaching role for others may help to get some clarity for your own time utilisation.

Imagine yourself working with someone who is new to your business. You explain to them that there are no shortage of things to do and that they need to be clear about how to prioritise; because they cannot do everything, they must make sure that they spend their time doing those things which bring the results that they are expected to deliver and do those things which add most value. The Urgent and Important Matrix would be a fantastic tool to help them understand the importance of making some proactive decisions.

Most people know that they will need to spend a lot of time in the top right corner of the matrix and at first glance many assume that this is where they should put most focus. They realise they are also likely to be pulled into the top left box, by other people's bad planning and disorganisation, and they could probably see for themselves that the bottom left is the least productive. However, they may need some nudging to really think about the bottom right box, which of course is where they should continually strive to spend more time.

Truly proactive people will understand the theory that (like a pilot of a Jumbo 747) it is sensible to get into the bottom right hand box and to deal with things that are important **before they become urgent** ... but the stumbling block for many people is to understand **how** to get there, which I will demonstrate below.

Prioritising the boxes

Number the boxes on the Urgent and Important Matrix as follows:

- ☐ **Important not Urgent** **Box 1**
- ☐ **Urgent and Important** **Box 2**
- ☐ **Urgent not Important** **Box 3**
- ☐ **Neither Urgent nor Important** **Box 4**

and look again at the Daily Task Tracker on page 84, where column 2 (the only column we have not really looked at thus far) is headed Box 1-4.

We now have a language to use to refer to the different quality of tasks that have been recorded on the Tracker.

Remember, Box 1 (bottom right) tasks are proactive and it is worth working hard to find them a space in our plans – while at the other extreme, Box 4 tasks (bottom left) are low value and any time spent on them is simply time spent keeping busy.

When you have made some notes about how you spend your time, notice how many tasks from each box you have recorded.

Now that we have a language to describe the hierarchy of value of each task that is plotted on the matrix and recorded on the Daily Task Tracker and we can see that some tasks are more 'right' than others, it is a short step to plan to do more of some and less of others.

Achieving major tasks

In order to achieve major tasks, we need clarity.

The John Nabers story (page 76) showed how important it is to have a goal and forge a series of links between the distant aspiration at one extreme and small tangible 'things to do' on the way to achieving it, at the other.

Whether he knew it or not, Nabers was actually applying a logical project management technique – building a dam or organising a birthday party follow exactly the same principles, which are utilised by project management tools like Microsoft Project or the PERT system of planning. All are aimed at getting important tasks done, before they become urgent.

Eating salami

Tackling goals, projects and tasks can be like eating a whole salami. To eat it all at once or in a very short timescale would be overwhelming. Cutting it up into slices would make it more palatable and, interspersed amongst more mundane things, might even come to be seen as being appetising – something that adds spice and which can be looked forward to.

Case Study 14:

Eating salami

Dave was a successful entrepreneur who owned and ran a highly successful country house hotel and restaurant. He met with his management team and explained to them that because of the fantastic success of the business to date, he intended to expand the physical size of the property and wanted to explore the implications of building an extension with them.

As he announced his plan, his colleagues realised that although the design, building and fitting-out would be handled by external organisations, the project would inevitably have an impact on them and each of their departments from day one, all the way through to the day that the new wing was opened for business – after which, they realise that they would face fresh challenges from a business that would have the potential to attract a hugely increased customer base and revenue.

As a professional in the hospitality industry, Dave found the analogy of 'eating salami' a useful way to explain his ideas about the best way forward. He told his colleagues that the wall of their own ballroom would become the 'salami wall' and, he asked people to brainstorm (one idea per yellow sticky) all of the things that they would need to think about and do, if they were to address this challenge effectively.

The opening date was nine months away, so they took each panel on the wall to equate with one calendar month. The left hand side of panel one was their start date – where the first yellow sticky would be placed, and the right hand side of panel nine was their finishing date – where the last yellow sticky would be placed.

They brainstormed all of the other yellow stickies into the space in between.

As they got involved, everyone quickly realised how big and diverse the project was, but they also saw how groups of yellow stickies seemed to cluster together naturally. They saw periods where there would need to be a lot of activity. They saw bottlenecks and areas of inactivity, as well as opportunities where several parts of the project could be running simultaneously.

People got really excited as they could visualise where they and their departments fitted into this big picture. They could scope the shape and flow of the work that was needed and some of them went off to get members of their own teams, so that they could use the wall and Dave's picture language to explain this project to their colleagues.

Once responsibilities were given for small areas of the project, individuals came to see that these sub-projects or tasks could be treated as salami too. For example, a simple task falling to the sales and marketing lead, (to make a presentation to the board in a month and a half's time), could be planned using exactly the same principles.

When looking at a sub-project the temptation is to say that "This is only a small salami. I'm used to making presentations and I do not have to make it for another six weeks", but of course the perspective here is wrong.

The date that would go into most people's planning system is the date of delivery, whereas, in fact, there are several stages and a lot of planning, preparation (some involving other people) and practice involved prior to the event, if they are to be able to deliver a well thought-through and well-rehearsed marketing presentation.

An initial action plan for the marketing presentation might be as set out in the following Action Planning Pro-forma (Figure 28). (See Appendix 3 for a blank version of this pro-forma.)

Action Planning Pro-forma

Who, needs to do what, by when?!

Presentation to the board to get permission to progress Proj. X		
Who	**What**	**When**
JS	Gather written data	
MJ	Gather & confirm financials	
TM	Gather visuals (ppt & technical diagrams)	
MJ PR DP RB	Meet with project team i) confirm programme	
	ii) Agree presentation	
MB	First draft of presentation	
JS PR CS and...	Circulate	
MB	Second draft of presentation	
JM	Type & reproduce support documents	
MJ	Create supporting Ppt deck	
MB & MJ	Practice presentation	
	Deliver mind numbingly brilliant	
MB	presentation!	26:11:07
	Task received 15:10:07 ← 6 WEEKS!!	

Figure 28

In the example above, the task of creating and delivering the presentation about Project X was received by MB six weeks before the due date. At that stage, all that he knew was that he had a presentation to make, the date that the task was received and the date for completion. It is understandable that he might put it to one side, thinking that he had more pressing things to do now and plenty of time to tackle this at a later date.

However a logical and more useful approach would be to brainstorm the component parts of the task and to begin to allocate responsibility and deadlines for each. The key to this is to start at the bottom of the sequenced brainstormed activities – i.e. with the delivery of the presentation, and for MB to work backwards in his planning towards today's date.

In order to be ready to deliver on the 26/11/07, the typing and reproduction and the PowerPoint presentation all need to be ready. Experience suggests this will take JM about four hours to complete.

It might be tempting for MB to delegate this task to JM four hours before the presentation is due(!) and expect her to be able to do it there and then. This is a great example of pushing a colleague into the top left hand box (Box 2) on the Urgent and Important Matrix, (see Figure 27). Actually, having a conversation with JM *today* (15/10/07), will help MB to understand her availability and enable her to find a space for the tasks in her plans.

By having a conversation, MB is reminded that JM has booked holiday for two weeks beginning on 19/11/07 and so she will actually need to receive this task in the week commencing 12/11/07 and, while she agrees that she can probably turn it around in about four hours, her first opportunity to start will not be until the 13/11/07.

This helps MB to understand that his second draft of the presentation needs to be completed by the 12/11/07. So, he should ask himself *today* (15/10/07) where does he have the necessary four or five hours to do his second draft of the presentation in time to hand it over to JM by 13/11/07? Let us say that on this occasion, by referring to his diary, he finds he has some space on 06/11/07. He books an appointment with himself ***right now*** for when he is going to do this work.

This means that he needs to have received back his circulated first draft by 06/11/07. Again, experience says it will take a couple of days to reach each of his colleagues and a couple of days for them to do something with it – he will allow six days in his plans, but tell them that they only have four(!). This means he needs to have his first draft completed by Friday 26/10/07. He is away himself all of that week (it's half-term) and so he will need to create the first draft in the week commencing 15/10/07.

That's today!

His diary for this week is already full! He needs to gather the data, the visuals, meet with the project team, agree the content and make a space to make the first draft of his presentation today.

He is about to be caught out by this presentation salami and it dawns on him that this apparently low priority task, that he 'could get round to any time', is actually rather more urgent than he had at first thought, so he must re-prioritise his plans and find a space in his diary when he can do it.

Key points

- ❑ **Spot the salami early.** Recognise it for what it is – something that you want to achieve and which is worthy of your attention.
- ❑ **Be clear about how big the salami is** – when it is a long way away it looks small and easy to deal with. Have you noticed the closer you get to the date a goal or a task must be completed the bigger and more overwhelming it can become?
- ❑ **Divide the salami into manageable slices** – in other words scope it out. What has to happen, by when?
- ❑ **Decide when you are going to start and finish each part of the whole.**
- ❑ **Find out if there is anybody who can eat some of the salami for you** – this is called delegating!
- ❑ **Decide if there is a logical order in which to eat different parts** – can some bits be mixed with other things to make them more pleasant?
- ❑ **Commit to working on it** – decide where it will fit into your plans – if it is not worthy of a space in your calendar, it will not happen.
- ❑ **Start working on it** – keep working on it.
- ❑ **Stick to the plan.**
- ❑ **But ... do not be afraid to change to a Plan B, if necessary** – be strong ... only change it if the new plan is suitable and effective.

Getting into Box 1...

So, where does eating salami fit on the Urgent and Important Matrix? When a task is apparently small and a long way away, it is important, but not yet urgent (Box 1). These sorts of tasks gather together in the bottom right hand box.

The mistake that many people make with salami on the horizon is to focus on the end date, the date by which the task needs to be completed, and because this is often some way off, they are able to convince themselves that they do not need to start just yet!

The real value of the salami technique is that it helps the salami eater to spot the salami early, to scope out just how great a challenge it really is going to be and to break it down into smaller, more manageable pieces – each of which have deadlines and implications for how everybody involved in the task will need to allocate their time.

...and out again!

A few minutes thinking through these implications will enable most people to realise that in order to hit the final deadline, they will need to get some time booked into their own and other people's diaries. In other words, they realise that some of the component parts of the task do not actually live in the bottom right hand box (Box 1) at all; they are more sensibly located in the top right hand box, **both Urgent and Important** (Box 2), a box where many people claim that they already spend most of their time!

Some parts of the salami have always been both Urgent and Important. It is just that until applying the salami technique, the salami eater could remain blissfully unaware how urgent it was to get started! What the salami technique does is to help the salami to move into Box 2!

Having gone through the planning process described above, do not feel despondent – you have no additional work to do – but you **do** have clarity about how big the task is and are better positioned to enhance your effectiveness by planning realistically and proactively – deciding what (on this occasion) you can and cannot do, how you can allocate resources and who you need to tell!

In order to get through tasks, it is important to break them into their component parts and to position them realistically on the Urgent and Important Matrix. Each and every component part will demand an investment of time (not just the delivery date) and must be allocated a place in the diary. Inevitably, this means that the diary will fill up with things to do and, when there is no more space, it is obvious that to find additional capacity some re-planning will need to be done.

Using the salami technique in this way means that the diary is likely to contain a higher proportion of proactive tasks that need to be done and rather fewer appointments made for other peoples' benefit. Now, if anyone requests diary space for a meeting you will both find that your diary is already full – you will also be able to see the comparative opportunity cost of saying "Yes" to other peoples' requests and although you may choose to change your plans, you can do so in the knowledge that you can see the opportunity cost of being deflected.

Chapter 5

Questioning What You Do

- Core roles and responsibilities
- Re-aligning roles and responsibilities
- Core areas of activity
- Re-aligning core areas of activity
- Application 1
- Application 2
- Application 3
- Application 4

Core roles and responsibilities

What roles do you currently fulfil?

Using the diagram below, make a note of the roles that you currently have within your business. What 'hats' do you wear at work?

Are you a manager or supervisor? Do you have mentoring or coaching responsibilities? Do you train others? Are you a fire warden or first aider? Do you sit on planning or organising committees? Do you play the role of 'agony aunt', motivator, social event organiser?

Let your mind run free and notice how many diverse roles you actually have.

Figure 29

There will be some roles that you have listed that you did not 'sign up' to, but which came with the job and which carry with them a degree of responsibility and a set of expectations from others.

Now, think about your private life. What 'hats' do you wear at home?

Are you someone's partner, son, daughter or grandchild? Do you have parental responsibilities? Are you someone's best friend? Are you responsible for finances or maintenance? Do you provide a taxi service?

Again there will be some roles that you have listed that you did not knowingly sign up to, but each of them come with a degree of responsibility and a set of expectations from others, who will each have an opinion about how you should be allocating your time.

Finally, think about your community. What 'hats' do you wear in that space between work and home?

Are you a school governor? Are you on the PTA, a local council or any other group? Do you get involved in charity work or fundraising? Do you have a passion, a sport or a hobby that involves you taking on an organising role or investing large amounts of your time? Are you someone who chairs meetings, acts as treasurer or secretary or do you contribute by giving your time and energy?

As before, there will be some roles that you have listed that you almost fell into and are doing by default, but each carries responsibility and a set of expectations from others, who will feel free to comment on your skill and level of commitment!

As you review your headings, it may occur to you that some of these roles are more important to you than others. Think back over the last year, and check back in your diary and other planning tools. Which of these roles have had the biggest call on your time? In retrospect, are you spending your time on the 'right' things or are some individuals, groups or aspects of your life claiming a disproportionately large space in your plans, because they shout out louder than others and as a result get a first claim on the space in your diary?

Re-aligning roles and responsibilities

Use the diagram below to identify your core, your Level 2 and your Level 3 roles.

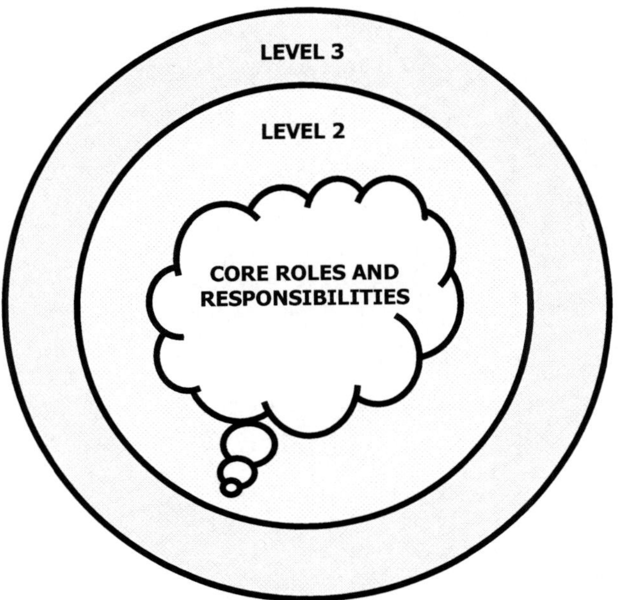

Figure 30

How can you proactively realign your roles, responsibilities and time allocation?

____

____

____

Core areas of activity

In Chapter 4, we used the Daily Task Tracker to record how you actually spent your time at work. This data can now be used to identify your core areas of activity.

Take a separate piece of paper and list the things that you do day-to-day and week-to-week down one side. You can easily grow this list by letting your mind run free – imagine that you had completed the Daily Task Tracker at two or three different times during the year. What other things might you have recorded? What are the things that take your time on an irregular or cyclical basis? Try to list as much as you can – the more you list, the better the outcome will be.

Using highlighter pens to colour-code, group 'like with like'. As you generate clusters of activity, give each a group name. These each represent one of your current core areas of activity.

The headings that you create will be specific to you and your job function and obviously if you changed your job, your list of core activities would be different. A common list might include such headings as:

- ❑ staff
- ❑ business development
- ❑ personal development
- ❑ finance
- ❑ projects
- ❑ budgets
- ❑ health and safety
- ❑ communications
- ❑ knowledge updating
- ❑ administration
- ❑ expenses

Re-aligning core areas of activity

When you have created this list, you may want to store it somewhere where you will be able to refer to it, because it has a few applications.

Application 1

Look at each core activity heading that you have created.

How much time **do you currently** spend on each core activity?
(Proportion of time / hours)

____

____

____

How much time **should you** spend on each core activity?
(Proportion of time / hours)

____

____

____

How much time **would you like** to spend on each core activity?
(Proportion of time / hours)

____

____

____

Where are the differences?

____

____

____

What proactive core activities are missing?

Would these headings have been the same last year?

Will they need to be the same next year?

Application 2

Once you have this list established, refer to it occasionally and ensure that you are planning to do something proactive in each of your core areas of activity and more importantly, that you are not being drawn towards fighting fires (see Chapter 1) in one core area, at the expense of others.

Application 3

You may like to compare your list of core areas of activity with the folder or directory headings that you use to organise your files in both Word and Outlook. What you have created with this list is a 'top line' index of what you actually do – and for this reason there should be some strong correlations with your PC folders. However, as you may engage in some activities that have no connection at all with your desk-based or laptop systems, it will not necessarily be an exact match.

Application 4

Proactive results-oriented planning means that even though you have the same job title, your core activities may well change from year to year. True results-oriented planning is based on identifying goals (Chapter 3), identifying the tasks that you need to work on (Chapter 4), and then implementing the plan, using the most appropriate tools (Chapter 2).

Take some time to look at your goals. Remind yourself of the dream. Look at the performance measures and check that you are working on the process goals.

Look at your core roles and responsibilities. Are you doing something in each of these? How have they changed and how are they likely to change in the future?

Now, look at your core areas of activity. Have you found the right amount of space for each of these in your plans?

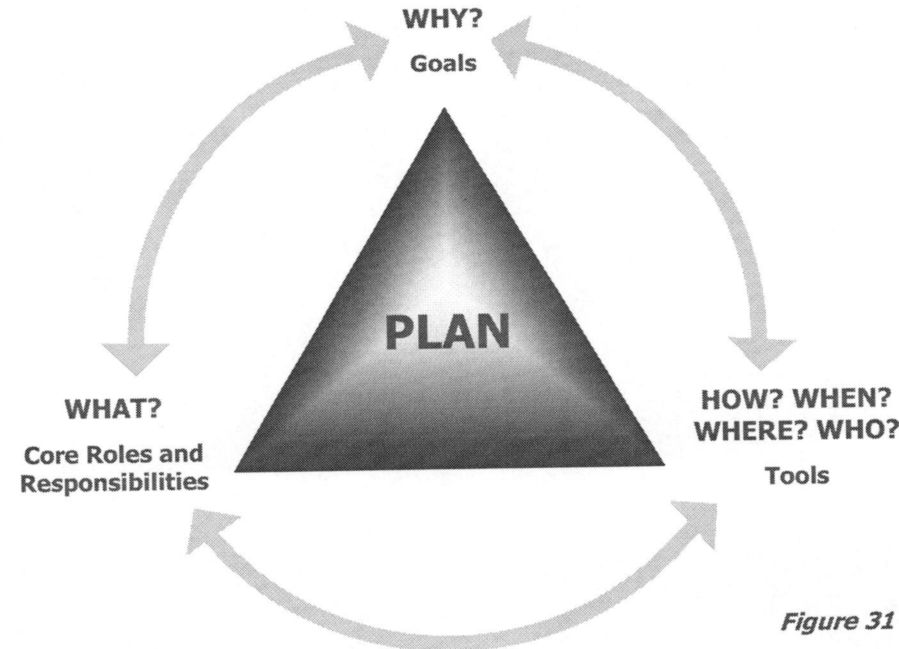

Figure 31

Chapter 6

Managing Delegated Tasks

- Managing people
- Guidelines for delegation
- Keeping good records
- The 5 faces of delegation
- Delegating to the right person
- Case Study 15
- Tasks Delegated To Pro-forma
- Looking for opportunity
- Guidelines for delegators
- Putting theory into practice
- Guidelines for subordinates

Chapter 6 – Managing Delegated Tasks

Managing people

Managing is about getting things done through people, and it is therefore incumbent upon managers to manage, monitor and manipulate the delegation process.

Delegation is an essential activity that managers must proactively engage with and there is no doubt that those who are successful, manage themselves and the people that they work with in such a way that that both the organisation and the people benefit from their presence.

Managers do not have to do everything themselves – they do not have to carry the world on their shoulders!

Practising delegation frees a manager's own time, enabling them to be more productive and creative. It establishes the manager and their subordinates as a team and allows room for professional growth – which is beneficial for everyone.

Unfortunately, because the delegation process requires an initial commitment of time and energy on the part of delegators (as they define the tasks to be handed over and then give necessary instruction and possibly training to complete those tasks), it is inevitable that managers who seek to delegate may find time and attention taken away from the functional things that they still need to do.

Guidelines for delegation

In order to delegate properly, a manager must think and plan ahead, spot major tasks on the horizon, decide who will do what, by when, and communicate their thinking to the people they are delegating to. Only then will their subordinates be able to incorporate what may well be a simple task for the manager, but which might feel like a huge task to the subordinates, into their plans.

Managers will need to:

- ❑ assign responsibilities to the right people.
- ❑ outline projects and tasks clearly and check for understanding.
- ❑ be very clear about their expectations (the timescales, reporting processes and the required outcomes).
- ❑ agree the nature and extent of authority required for each of their tasks to be completed.
- ❑ delegate interesting and rewarding tasks, as well as the dull and uninspiring ones.
- ❑ ensure that individuals are sufficiently trained to be able to deliver to standard and on time.

Keeping good records

Establish a method that suits you to keep good records of all of the tasks that are delegated. These should be specific to each subordinate, but should also allow comparison with the tasks delegated to other subordinates.

The 'Tasks Delegated To' pro-forma (Figure 33) offers some ideas of the sort of things that need to be recorded and which will help to track progress.

Having assigned delegated tasks, it is important that the manager is able to stand back from them. Not doing so will imply that they have a lack of trust or confidence in their subordinates' ability to deliver.

Conversely, if things do not run to plan, managers must be equally ready to intervene, to facilitate a successful outcome. Good records will allow the manager to monitor from a distance.

Do not be tempted to use records as a means to catch people doing something wrong. Use them to proactively manage an individual's performance and to catch them doing something right! Having good records will make it much easier to coach performance in the short term and to have good data for appraisals or the PDP process in the longer term.

Keeping good records allows managers to check progress, as well as reminding them to celebrate success.

The delegation process can be seen as a sort of contract between manager and subordinate; if handled properly, it should never be viewed by either party as an abdication of the manager's responsibilities.

What are the benefits of delegating?

____

____

____

In your experience, what stops people from delegating?

____

____

____

What are **your** personal barriers to delegation?

Make a list of the problems that you have experienced when other people delegate to **you**.

What lessons can you learn from this, to ensure that in future delegation to you is improved?

What lessons can you learn from this in order to improve your own delegation skills?

The 5 faces of delegation

Everyone understands that it is important to delegate the right things to the right people. So, which are the right things?

We began to look for opportunities to delegate in the previous chapter, using the Daily Task Tracker and the 4 D's. A further tool to help identify which tasks to delegate is the '5 faces of delegation', illustrated below.

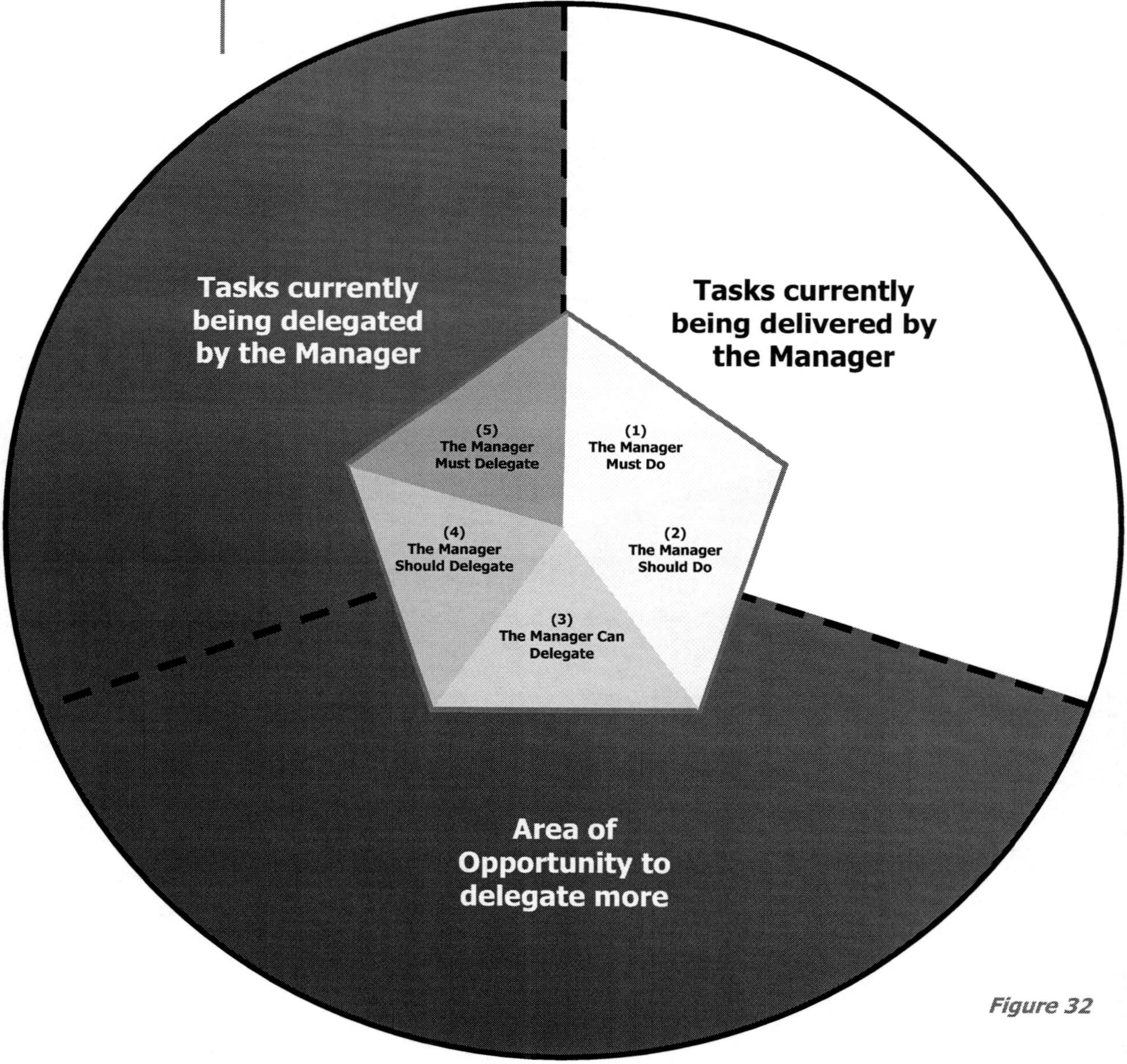

Tasks currently being delegated by the Manager

Tasks currently being delivered by the Manager

(5) The Manager Must Delegate

(1) The Manager Must Do

(4) The Manager Should Delegate

(2) The Manager Should Do

(3) The Manager Can Delegate

Area of Opportunity to delegate more

Figure 32

(1) Tasks which the manager MUST deal with.

The sort of things that this section might contain are:

- the implementation of strategies.
- policing of policies and budgets.
- the management of direct reports, including:
    - recruitment and dismissal of staff.
    - the appraisal and PDP process.
    - showing recognition.
    - mentoring and coaching.
    - managing the disciplinary process.
- delivering fundamental tasks where they hold particular expertise or perhaps where their knowledge can add value in other parts of the business.

Create your own list of Must Do tasks below:

____

____

____

(2) Tasks which the manager SHOULD deal with.

These fall into two main groups:

- Major or complicated tasks which are best dealt with by the manager, perhaps for procedural or political reasons, although in delivering them they may usefully draw support and expertise from others.
- Tasks which can only be delegated in situations where the deadlines are proximate, or where there are other reasons for great urgency and when the task simply needs to be done!

Create your own list of Should Do tasks below:

____

____

____

(3) Tasks which the manager CAN delegate.

This is obviously the most important area for managers – and it is a fantastic area of opportunity. These are tasks which are best dealt with by the manager – but which other staff can deal with, given a certain amount of training, guidance and encouragement.

In the short term the manager will usually be able to perform these tasks more quickly and perhaps to a higher standard than the delegated person is able to.

Any time spent here should be seen by the manager as an investment, which in the long run is worthwhile – the pay-off being less time pressure and a release of capacity to deal with their other proactive tasks, which might include personal development, staff development or administering more delegated tasks!

It may also be that delegating 'stretch' tasks to able and ambitious performers will be part of the manager's own PD and progression planning.

Tasks in this type of delegation will benefit particularly from close management and monitoring by the line manager, who may well need to adopt the role of coach to facilitate success.

Create your own list of Can Delegate tasks below:

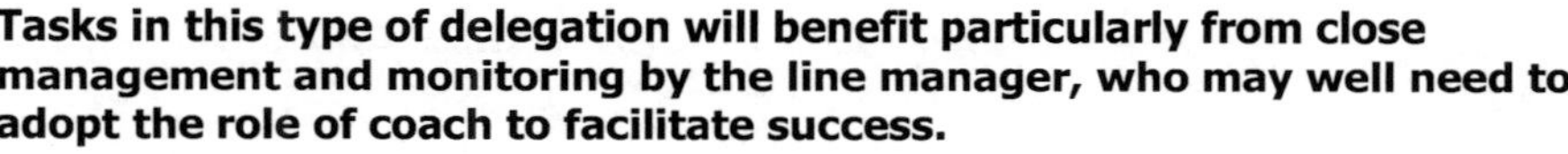

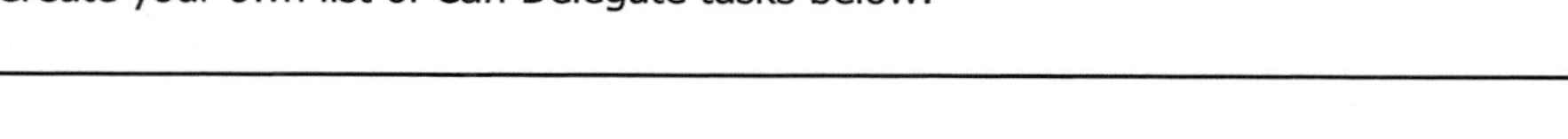

Initially, there are likely to be errors and misunderstanding – frustrating for all concerned! It may feel like it is much easier for the manager to give up and to do it themselves than to keep going. Don't be tempted!

(4) Tasks which the manager SHOULD delegate.

SHOULD DELEGATE

The sort of things that this section might contain are:

- ❑ tasks which need to be completed, irrespective of whether the manager is available or not.
- ❑ tasks which can be dealt with in the appropriate manner and to the appropriate standard, without the manager's direct involvement.
- ❑ tasks which demand a quick or flexible response, if the organisation is to function properly.
- ❑ any task for which the staff have the competence (given the information, the training and the necessary guidelines).

Create your own list of Should Delegate tasks below:

____

____

____

(5) Tasks which the manager MUST delegate.

MUST DELEGATE

The sort of things that this section might contain are:

- ❑ tasks which are a natural part of the work of staff and which may appear in their job description.
- ❑ tasks which do not need the manager's direct involvement or sign-off in order to be completed.
- ❑ tasks which staff can perform faster, better or perhaps to a higher quality than the manager.
- ❑ tasks which consist only of implementing or putting in place decisions that have been made elsewhere.

Create your own list of Must Delegate tasks below:

____

____

____

Delegating to the right person

For delegation to be effective, the manager must be aware of each subordinate's ability and motivation levels, which obviously decide the degree to which they can operate independently.

The manager then needs to be able to adjust their delegation approach for different people and with different tasks, accordingly.

Case Study 15:

Delegation choices

> Cal has two colleagues. One always delivers to the right standard and on time. The other is rather more high-maintenance and needs to be nudged, encouraged, cajoled, reminded and told to complete delegated tasks.
>
> Cal is under pressure and has tasks that he needs to delegate immediately. Who should he delegate them to?

We all understand the theory of delegation, but the reality is that we also want to be sure that a delegated task will be completed, as requested. The temptation for Cal may well be to ask the colleague who always comes through – let's call her Jan – to take on this new task. But what signal is he giving to his other colleague, Jim?

Although it is hard and will take more of his time, Cal should put his role of manager and developer above his need to get the task completed and should allocate time to proactively drive the delegation process.

Cal must recognise and reward the behaviour that he wants to encourage and demand more from his under-performing colleague, rather than heaping more tasks onto Jan, who is doing a good job, but who may begin to think that she is being taken for granted.

It is really important that Cal finds a way to be alerted to the fact that delegated tasks have been completed – only then will he be able to develop his subordinates' independent willingness to take on additional tasks. For a manager to know that a subordinate is thinking "I can do that," is a confirmation that they are positioned to take on tasks with a degree of confidence that signals the delegation process is working effectively.

Have you ever worked hard on a delegated task and when you have completed it, no-one has noticed? How motivational was that for you? Catch people doing something right and they are more likely to be willing to tackle the task with energy and enthusiasm the next time.

Whenever a meeting takes place between managers and staff at which tasks are delegated, it is important that the tasks delegated are recorded. It will take just a moment to capture them, but by having a note and reviewing it occasionally, appropriate follow-up is much more likely.

It may sound cynical, but often what gets checked gets done. Certainly, if delegates know that there will be follow-up they are more likely to keep their eye on the ball.

Tasks Delegated To Pro-forma

Tasks delegated to: Jan.

Who	Action Required	Priority	Date of Meeting	Due by	✓
	Mark – walkways and report back.	(A)	22:10:07	30:10:07	
	Amend task acc. to the new.	(B)	23:10:07	14:11:07	
	Establish area – new parameter.	(C)	25:10:07	30:10:07 14:11:07	#1 #2

For a blank version of this pro-forma, see Appendix 4

Figure 33

It might be good to agree a convention to distinguish between different types of delegated tasks. In the example above:

- ❑ **A Type Tasks** are those where manager and delegated subordinate agree that the subordinate has everything that they need (the ability, time, energy, resource...) to complete the task delegated and they are just expected to have completed it to standard on or before the date agreed.
- ❑ **B Type Tasks** are also within the subordinate's sphere of influence, but as they may be part of a larger project involving the manager, the subordinate is expected to complete them to standard on or before the date agreed and then to report back to their manager.
- ❑ **C Type Tasks** can be seen as more of a stretch for the person delegated – they may not have everything they need to complete the task and so will require more support from their manager, who should use the first deadline date as a reminder that they should begin to check for progress, so that they can offer support and encouragement as necessary, to facilitate success.

It is also important for the manager to use the 'due by' column. Periodically, they should scan down and look for deadlines coming up over the next few weeks – this acts as a reminder to praise, chase, or if the task is complex and likely to be deferred by a subordinate, to check whether they have started and what support they will need to achieve it.

The delegator can use this pro-forma:

- ❑ to keep an overview of how many and what level of delegated tasks they are expecting each of their subordinates to deliver.
- ❑ as a prompt to remind themselves to 'catch people doing something right'.
- ❑ to help with appraisals, reviews and 1:1s, by providing the overview data needed to identify who is performing well and in which areas.

The delegated subordinate can use this pro-forma:

- ❑ as a record to ensure that there is no misunderstanding about what is expected of them, and by when.
- ❑ at appraisal, as evidence of what has, or has not been achieved through an appraisal period.

Remember, it is in the manager's interest that delegated tasks are completed on time and to standard, by people who feel **able** to do the task and as a result will be more likely to take on the task even more readily the next time.

Looking for opportunity

For a specific task, ask yourself:

- ❑ Is there someone who can do the task better than I can? Am I really utilising the potential, experience or expertise of my staff?
- ❑ Is there someone who, while doing the task slightly differently from me, or who by taking slightly more time, could still achieve an acceptable level of output?
- ❑ Is there someone who is paid less than me, who can do the task satisfactorily, thus lowering the cost of achieving the task?
- ❑ If I cannot do the task today, is there someone else who can?
- ❑ Is there someone for whom this task may be a stretch, but who would benefit from the experience of working on it and/or achieving it as part of their personal development?

If the answer to any of these questions is "YES" – get delegating!!

Delegation is essentially a proactive task, demanding careful thought and planning at the front end, close monitoring and management in the middle and appropriate follow-up at the conclusion.

Guidelines for delegators

Delegators should:

- ❑ **Proactively look for opportunities to delegate** – which they can only do successfully if they are able to plan ahead.
- ❑ **Decide who to delegate to** – either match the person with the task, because it is within their comfort zone and current sphere of expertise, or use it as a stretch task, an opportunity to develop an individual. How well this is balanced has obvious implications for the degree of management involvement, and the decision of what to delegate to whom has implications on how the process needs to be managed.
- ❑ **Agree the delegation contract and make sure that all parties are clear** – is this an A, B or C delegated task? (See Figure 33.)
- ❑ **Remember to delegate the good and the bad, the mundane and the stretch** – each delegated task should be part of a bigger, balanced plan.
- ❑ **Specify and agree the required outcomes** – confirm the subordinate's understanding is the same as yours.
- ❑ **Keep in touch** – this is delegation, not abdication!
- ❑ **Keep good records** – and follow-up.

Putting theory into practice

Choose five tasks from your own work situation, which could be delegated. Put together a delegation plan for each.

Proactive and developmental delegation planning should include:

1. **Details of the task** – the scope of responsibility; core areas in which results are to be accomplished; specific objectives; time scales.
2. **An outline of the result to be achieved** and an explanation of the quantitative and qualitative measures that will be used.
3. **Details of the person** – their existing abilities; their level of interest and motivation; their time availability and any previous training and previous experience.
4. **The training needed to facilitate success** – method; cost; timing.
5. **The feedback mechanism** – milestones; method; frequency.
6. **Your own responsibilities** – as delegator.
7. **A balanced task distribution** – make sure that you have a mix of tasks for each individual and a fair balance across the whole team.

Guidelines for subordinates

If you are not getting delegated to in the way that you might wish, there may be some proactive actions that you can take:

- ❑ **Do not accept:**
  - unclear instructions.
  - too many projects that have to be handled simultaneously.
  - ill-defined deadlines.
- ❑ **Never be afraid to ask for an order of priority** – which task needs to be completed first, which second?
- ❑ **When you receive delegated tasks** – summarise and repeat them back in your own words to ensure that you and the delegator have the same 'picture' of success.
- ❑ **Ask for specific deadlines** and reporting stages for each part of the project.
- ❑ **Clarify the quality level and any other measures.**
- ❑ **Clarify your own level of authority** – getting this right means that you will not have to constantly go back to check for approval from your boss.
- ❑ **As problems arise, discuss them with your boss** – along with your suggestions as to the best way forward. This shows that your independence and motivation levels are high – you are using your initiative, thinking creatively and driving towards positive solutions.

Do not be tempted to volunteer for tasks and then complain that you have too much to do!

Remember – intelligent people learn from their mistakes – as well as their successes!

Everyone benefits from mentoring, coaching and empowerment.

Chapter 7

Managing Meetings

- Too many meetings
- Meetings Pro-forma
- Improving meetings 1
- Effective participation
- Effective meetings
- Improving meetings 2
- Improving meetings 3
- Behaviours in meetings
- Productive participants
- Keeping meetings short
- Making use of technology: Audio conferencing, Video conferencing, Live Meeting and Instant Messaging

Too many meetings

Meetings are essential to the communicating and decision-making process – but to be worthwhile they must be effective for all of the participants.

Before you agree to a meeting, P-A-U-S-E.

Always ask:

- ❑ **Do I need to attend this meeting?**
  - Where does this meeting fit into my priorities? Will the benefit derived from attending be worth the investment of my time?
  - What will attending this meeting prevent me from doing?
- ❑ **If I do attend, what are my objectives and ideal outcomes from doing so?**
- ❑ **Has an agenda been published** – and if it has, would it be useful to study it in advance?
- ❑ **What else do I need to do to prepare?** – is there anything that needs to be added to the agenda? Is it necessary for me to prepare contributions and questions?

You may also want to confirm that all of the key players will be attending and that the outcomes set are achievable. If they are not, suggest that other people need to be invited, that the agenda needs to be revised or recommend a postponement.

Always question whether a face-to-face meeting is the best medium for you to action the objectives of your job and whether you *need* to attend. Ask yourself:

- ❑ **How does this meeting fit into my day?** Would it save time if I hosted the meeting – and so avoid travelling to someone else's office? This has the added benefit that you are more likely to be able to drive the agenda and dictate how long the meeting will run.
- ❑ **If I do have to travel** – what else could I plan to do on the way to it or on the way back that would enable me to make the most of my time? Can I take the opportunity to organise a supplementary meeting with some of the participants whilst I am in the same location?

Be ruthless in your time planning – if the pain of attending is not worth the gain, find an alternative!

Put value on your own and other people's time – do not spend £1,000 on a £100 decision!

- [ ] **Could you:**
  - send a representative?
  - ask another attendee to brief you after the event?
  - organise a telephone or Video conference?
  - use email or Live Meeting?

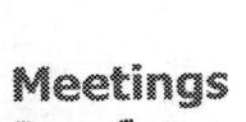

If your company has open access to diaries, be aware that other people may perceive gaps in your diary to be time when you are 'available' for meetings with them.

Protect yourself by booking 'meetings with yourself', before anyone else can get the chance to access your diary.

- [ ] **If you do accept a meeting:**
  - set aside the necessary time and be punctual.
  - prepare thoroughly.
  - make the most of the meeting when you are there.

Meetings Pro-forma

Consider using the Meetings Pro-forma below to ensure best practice is observed. The three columns on this document enable the capture of the information that is needed before, during and after the meeting. (For a blank version of this pro-forma, see Appendix 5.)

Column 1	Column 2	Column 3
BEFORE THE MEETING: Use this column **Meeting:** to circulate, who when where & what information	AT THE MEETING: Use this **Notes** column for notes	AFTER THE MEETING: Use this **Action Plan** column to record actions agreed
Date: 22:10:07 **Time:** 10.00 – 11.00 **Place:** RM 31 **People:** JS PR, JM CS, TM PB		**Who?** / **What?** / **When?** JS – 25:10:07 TM – 29:10:07 PB & CS – 25:10:07 PR
Agenda: 1 2 3 4 5 6 7 8 AOB		

Figure 34

The chairperson should begin by reviewing Column 1 and confirming the purpose of the meeting – is it for communications, feedback, reporting, updating, policy, planning, crisis limitation...? This will affect how participants will need to behave. It is then smart to review the agenda in order to prioritise it, re-order it, to allocate time to each component and to confirm the proposed finishing time. Ask for everyone's agreement (i.e. make a contract) before starting.

Improving meetings

Be aware of:

- ❑ **The chairperson** – do they have the correct skills? (These do not always come with seniority!) Should other roles be allocated?
- ❑ **The location** – will the venue be conducive to holding an effective meeting? Is there a plan to avoid interruptions?
- ❑ **The time** – what time of day is best for you and the kind of meeting that you need? Could you agree short time limits on all or part of the meeting?

Remember to allow sufficient time for breaks and the regeneration of energy. Always begin by asking for phones to be switched off and laptop lids to be down.

If you want to improve your meetings, question:

- ❑ **What is a good size for this kind of meeting?**
  - Who needs to attend?
  - Can numbers be limited?
  - Should everyone stay for the whole meeting?
- ❑ **If it is a regular meeting – is it still necessary?**
  - Are meetings too frequent, or infrequent?
  - Could meetings be combined, or split?
- ❑ **Could you change the style or format of the meeting** – have 'stand-up' meetings, find ways to get people involved, use brainstorms...?

Meetings are most effective when:

- ❑ **there is a strong chairperson.**
- ❑ **the purpose of the meeting is made clear** beforehand and participants come prepared with all of the relevant information.
- ❑ **there are clear time parameters** for the start and finish and there is appropriate time budgeted for each agenda item.
- ❑ **contributions are focused** and limited to those which is useful and relevant.
- ❑ **attendance is restricted** to people affected by the issues under discussion.
- ❑ **the objectives of the meeting are seen to be achieved** and decisions are made and actions are owned and initiated.

Meetings are seen as ineffective when they:

- ❑ **appear to have no real purpose.**
- ❑ **make straightforward issues complicated.**
- ❑ **last too long.**
- ❑ **provide a platform for the talkative.**
- ❑ **delay decisions and actions.**

Every meeting should end by asking the question:

***"What is my action plan now?!"* – No action plan = No action!**

Improving meetings 1

Put three flip chart sheets on to the walls, headed:

- ❑ "How to sabotage a meeting."
- ❑ "How to undermine the chairperson."
- ❑ "How to avoid taking part in a meeting."

Give every participant a pack of yellow stickies and ask them to contribute three ideas to each chart, writing one idea per sticky. Then discuss the issues raised.

This should enable the participants to identify the key components which need to be in place for a meeting to be truly effective. From this, it is then possible to draw up two lists, one about **Effective Participation**, the other about **Effective Meetings**.

There are two samples over the page, (Figures 35 and 36) which could be used as checklists for future meetings – although there is more benefit in encouraging attendees of regular meetings to create lists specific to them, from which to score their own performance.

Effective participation

Meeting:	Date:		
Activity:	**Evaluation: ✓**		
	Yes	**No**	**Partially**
1. Did we all arrive on time so the meeting could start when planned?			
2. Were we prepared?			
3. Did we participate in a positive fashion?			
4. Did we listen to others?			
5. Did we address problems as 'how to' opportunities?			
6. Did we use paraphrasing and questions to ensure everyone's understanding?			
7. Did we give and accept feedback constructively?			
8. Did we respect the opinions of other participants?			
9. Did we talk about the present and avoid dwelling negatively on the past?			
10. Did we make suggestions and actively problem-solve?			
11. Did we support change?			
12. Did we avoid negative pre-judgements such as: 'that will never work'?			
13. Did we avoid assumptions and deal with facts?			
14. Did we empower the facilitator to manage the meeting when that was required?			

Figure 35

Effective meetings

Meeting:	**Date:**		
Activity:	**Evaluation:** ✓		
	Yes	**No**	**Partially**
1. Did the meeting start on time?			
2. Were there clear objectives?			
3. Was there a clear agenda?			
4. Was the agenda followed?			
5. Were expectations, roles and responsibilities clear?			
6. Was the meeting chaired and led effectively?			
7. Was the chairperson a positive role model?			
8. Did the chairperson explain *why*, as well as *what*, was to be done?			
9. Did the chairperson react appropriately to non-verbal communication?			
10. Did each attendee participate?			
11. Were specific tasks assigned when needed?			
12. Were opportunities, rather than problems, identified?			
13. Were problems phrased as 'how to' opportunities?			
14. Was paraphrasing used for clarification or summarising?			
15. Was active listening used?			
16. Were commitments asked for and made when needed?			
17. Were follow-up tasks established when needed?			
18. Was the time and place of the next meeting established (if necessary)?			
19. Was the meeting summarised?			
20. Did the meeting end on time or end early?			
21. Overall, did the meeting meet or exceed participants' expectations?			

Figure 36

Improving meetings 2

At the end of a regular meeting give each participant a sheet of A4 paper and a large pen and ask them to write on it a score out of ten for the meeting. This can be done in a light-hearted way and with no particular need for secrecy.

Ask everyone to show their paper simultaneously, so as to display the range of scores.

Ask each person in turn what would have to happen for them to have scored the meeting higher or for them to have been able to give a score of ten. Answers will usually vary, but they will give some ready pointers as to the sorts of areas that are currently causing frustration, but which might be addressed.

These could include:

❑ **Process issues** – things like:

- Not starting on time.
- Not finishing on time.
- Not sticking to or completing the agenda.

❑ **Content issues** – things like:

- Boring presentations.
- Poor use of visual aids.
- Lack of variety.

❑ **People issues** – things like:

- Lack of involvement.
- Individuals hijacking the agenda.
- Participants not listening to, or interrupting each other.
- People being distracted, because they or others are using laptops, mobile phones and instant messaging during the meeting.

Most of what needs to be done in order to have great meetings can be managed by a strong chairperson, supported by proactive meeting attendees.

There are many reasons why meetings may not work for the participants. Over the page are some common problems, with possible causes – along with pointers to solutions.

Improving meetings 3

- ❑ **The participants are uninformed about, or unaware of, the progress made during earlier meetings.**

Possible causes:

- Proper minutes have not been taken or, if they have been taken, have not been distributed.
- The minutes use jargon or abbreviations, which may make the content inaccessible to some participants.
- The minutes do not accurately describe the flow or the actions agreed in the meeting.

Possible solutions:

- Review the minute-taker's role and responsibilities.
- Ensure that the meeting minutes are well set out, are free of jargon and abbreviations, and that the minute-taker captures what was agreed, as much as what was said.
- Agree circulation lists and timescales – particularly how far in advance of the next meeting minutes will be made available to participants.

- ❑ **The meeting changes direction – apparently at random.**

Possible causes:

- The chairperson is weak.
- There is no agenda, or it is vague or poorly thought through.
- The goal of the meeting is unclear – is the meeting for the participants' information, is it intended as a forum for discussion, or is it an attempt to provide an opportunity for creative problem-solving ideas?
- There may need to be a number of different focuses to the meeting and the participants may need to be more (or less) involved at different stages – perhaps it is not clear to everyone when they should do what.
- All meetings follow a similar format – irrespective of the type of meeting, the number and level of attendees and the intended outcomes.

Possible solutions:

- Reconfirm the chairperson's role and the requirement for them to stay 'on track'.
- Define the format and the parameters of the meeting during planning and preparation. Set out and circulate a clear agenda in advance.
- Reconfirm the format and the parameters of the meeting at the start and ask everyone to agree that this is what will be happening.
- If participants want to change the agenda, be sure to involve everyone in the decision and get collective agreement to the change.
- Consider breaking diverse and confusing meeting content into a number of smaller meetings.

- ❑ **Chronic agenda changers.**

Possible causes:

- The agenda may not be clear and the chairperson may be weak.
- Participants may not feel involved in setting the agenda items and so are attempting to drive their own agenda.

Possible solutions:

- Confirm buy-in to the agenda by all participants at the start of the meeting.
- Invite people who want to have a different agenda to organise their own meeting.

- ❑ **Everyone switches roles, so no one knows who is doing what.**

Possible causes:

- Participants may not realise when they have a specific role to play.
- There is not a designated facilitator or chairperson or if there is, they do not manage the meeting or monitor the switching of roles.

Possible solutions:

- Review and agree roles, responsibilities and if necessary, behaviours.
- Rotate roles among participants over time, so that everyone shares the responsibility of chairing.
- Demonstrate respect and support for the chairperson.

- ❑ **Participants are not actively involved in the discussion.**

Possible causes:

- This may have its roots in history. Individuals may have previously offered many suggestions, but have learnt that they will be ignored, criticised or talked over.

Possible solutions:

- Help the chairperson to understand that if input is required, the process will need to be managed and people protected and encouraged by the chairperson – whose role may need to morph into that of a facilitator.
- Have participants agree 'good meetings practice' and to evaluate their own participation based on agreed behaviours. Use the Effective Meetings and Effective Participation checklists, (see Figures 35 and 36).
- Introduce alternative methods, aimed at involving people. Rather than allow 'free brainstorming' introduce a 'round-robin' format, where people offer ideas or response in turn.
- Give more recognition for input and suggestions and encourage people to build on each others ideas – perhaps using: 'Yes, and', rather than: 'Yes, but' language.

- **Finishing the meeting without covering the agenda.**

Possible causes:

- The agenda was too ambitious or was unrealistic in scope.
- There was inadequate preparation, facilitation or meeting management.
- A disproportionate amount of time was spent on the items that happened to be early on the agenda.
- There was poor personal time management displayed by all or some of the participants – the meeting started late, people were distracted, there were external interruptions...

Possible solutions:

- Be realistic about the time needed to deal with each agenda item and establish a start and finish time for each one – if each sub-deadline is not hit, the meeting will clearly either over-run or be incomplete at finishing time.
- Review the scope of every meeting. Invest time in setting agendas and in agreeing the content of the meeting, roles, responsibilities and timings at the outset.
- Highlight to the meeting attendees what is required for each agenda item – this is for information, to update, for review, for discussion and so on.
- Limit discussion time and keep debate focused. Drive for agreement on the required outputs, within the agreed timescales.
- Encourage good personal time management. If the meeting starts at 09.00, then a person arriving at 09.00 is not 'on time', they are late. Decide how this will be dealt with.

Leaders must give a lead and model good behaviour.

Behaviours in meetings

- **Some participants are intransigent, obstinate or stubborn.**

Possible causes:

- They may not be aware of all of the facts.
- They are overly committed to their own view and may need help with developing a 'selling' instead of 'telling' style.

Possible solutions:

- Help them to see the bigger picture and to see any parts that they might be able to agree with.
- Do not allow them to back themselves into a corner and pave the way for them to back down or to look for a compromise.
- Ask them: "What would have to happen for you to be willing to consider an alternative idea or outcome?"

- [ ] **Some participants are overly talkative.**

Possible causes:

- They may be naturally talkative, exceptionally well informed or keen to make their mark.
- They may see their role as being meeting leader, rather than meeting participant.

Possible solutions:

- Manage everyone's inputs and help them to understand the level of input that is required. Thank individuals for their contribution and say something like: "Okay, let's open this up to wider discussion..." or: "Shall we see if anyone has any alternative thoughts..."
- Encourage other people to speak, make eye contact and establish an order for contribution.
- Consider limiting the time available for individual inputs.
- If participants are talking over others (and are talking at the expense of listening), remind *everyone* that good meeting practice requires that only one person should be speaking at a time. Having made your point, you can then say something like: "Okay Al, why don't you go first and then we will hear from Muna and Christof..." or, "Okay, thanks for that – Liv what about you?" enabling other participants to take the floor.

- [ ] **Some participants tend to ramble, lose direction or seem to miss the point.**

Possible causes:

- It may be that they like the sound of their own voice or feel that they should have an opinion.
- It may be that they are abstract thinkers, or that they had thought about the subject incompletely, before engaging in dialogue.

Possible solutions:

- Introduce an idea and invite people to jot down their thoughts before launching into a dialogue.
- Establish a time limit for individual response.
- Introduce a round-robin for feedback – the chairperson can decide who to start with and can ask subsequent contributors to simply add any new thoughts or to say nothing, unless they have something new to add.
- If the response is abstract or tangential, the chairperson should ask the participant how their idea relates to the problem that is under discussion. If it does not, they should suggest 'parking it', while the current issue is worked upon. Remember to pick it up later.

- **Some participants are factually inaccurate.**

  Possible causes:

  - They have selective hearing or more likely have misunderstood the earlier facts.
  - They have been confused by jargon or TLAs (three letter acronyms)
  - They have pre-conceived ideas, based on inaccurate 'grapevine' information.

  Possible solutions:

  - Respectfully acknowledge their contribution, while correcting inaccurate information.
  - Clarify and reiterate the facts – make sure that everyone can distinguish the 'apples' from the 'oranges' – i.e. ensure that people are comparing like with like.

- **Some participants tend to moan or have other issues on their mind.**

  Possible causes:

  - They have a legitimate concern or there may be unresolved past conflict.
  - They are bringing other 'baggage' to this meeting.

  Possible solutions:

  - Confirm, and gain agreement on, the scope of the meeting and the agenda.
  - Confirm good meeting behaviour and practices.
  - Remind everyone of the need to stick to the agenda and suggest that unrelated issues should be dealt with in other forums.
  - If 'excess baggage' precludes an individual from taking a full and active part in the meeting, suggest that they might like to resolve their issues and then re-join the meeting.

- **Some participants are highly argumentative.**

  Possible causes:

  - They may feel that their ideas and opinions are not being heard and so they are becoming upset or combative.
  - They may have a separate or hidden agenda.
  - They may have particular interests, fears or stressors relating to the situation.

  Possible solutions:

  - Remind people that while this is an important, emotive or difficult subject, it is important that there should be dialogue and a free discussion.

- Encourage people to demonstrate good meetings practice, as well as the norms of politeness.
- Educate the group that saying 'but' negates saying 'yes'.

❑ **Some participants want to engage in side conversation.**

Possible causes:

- They may be discussing things unrelated to the meeting – either personal or business.
- They may be seeking clarification, sharing a creative idea or asking for more information.

Possible solutions:

- Stop talking, but make eye contact with them, whilst they are having their side conversation, until they stop.
- Ask if they are okay with the point under discussion and whether they have any other thoughts or comments that they think need to be aired.
- Check whether there is any unfinished business and ask if it is okay to move on.
- Remind the participants that it might be easier if the group could have one meeting at a time. Do not get cross – do be firm!

Productive participants

Participants have a major part to play in ensuring that all meetings are productive.

❑ **As a participant:**

- ask for an agenda at least a day in advance, so that you can prepare yourself for the meeting.
- be on time – if the meeting starts at 09.00, aim to arrive earlier:

  "To be early is to be on time.
  To be on time is to be late.
  To be late is unacceptable."

❑ **Ideal participants:**

- take responsibility and ensure they are in the right state of mind to contribute ideas and expertise.
- encourage others and seek consensus.
- stick with the agenda – keeping their comments brief and to the point and avoiding side conversations.
- help to create positive outcomes.

Keeping meetings short

Always begin a meeting by confirming when the target finishing time will be. This has particular value in 1:1 meetings, where it will help to plan out how the time available can best be spent.

Questioning the time available gives value to the meeting and it is important to emphasise that you want to do justice to it, but having an end time will instil a sense of urgency and create focus.

You can push this further by saying, "I could do with a quick meeting today". I have never encountered anyone who has said, "I would prefer to go for the full half day." Normally they say, "I could do with a quick meeting too," which makes it fast, focused and business like.

Some businesses push this further by having meetings standing up. Yo! Sushi, the restaurant chain, have a small meeting room where the only furniture is a high table for papers – no seating at all, thus encouraging energetic response! Other tricks are to have meetings running up to lunch or the end of the day.

In other businesses, good meetings practice has evolved through the use of video conferencing (see below). As video conferencing rooms can only be booked for a limited time, participants are incentivised to get in early to setup, are prepared and have clear agendas. They then work hard to keep to time – all vital ingredients for effective meetings.

Making use of technology:

Audio conferencing

By organising conference calls, individuals can save themselves and other meeting attendees vast amounts of travel time. If you need regular communications with disparate groups or need several diverse meetings in one day, then conference calling will become an invaluable tool. However, good meetings practice still applies – preparation, punctuality, being able to listen and to make your own contributions clearly and concisely will all be valued by others.

Because it is not possible to see the other participants in a conference call, it is easy to let standards of good meetings practice drop.

- ❑ It is imperative that you give the meeting your full attention.
- ❑ Do not be tempted to work on other things that are on your desk or to send emails during the meeting – the other participants will be able to tell – and although they may not challenge you, it will certainly affect how they view you and your commitment to the task in hand.
- ❑ Try to sit upright or even stand, in order to maintain energy in your voice.

As there are fewer clues to pick up, regular users of conference calling become very attuned to the other participants' level of contribution. Your voice and your contribution will give important clues as to whether you have turned up with your brain, as well as your body!

Everyone knows that you can 'hear a smile' and by thinking about and applying your energy and managing your posture, voice and facial expression, you can ensure that you will come across at your best.

Many businesses will have their own conferencing equipment. If you do not have access to such a set up, there are some fantastic providers on the web. A good example is PowWowNow at www.powwownow.co.uk.

This kind of conferencing service is 'free' – although every participant pays for the cost of a national or international rate phone call from wherever they are calling in order to take part.

Video conferencing

Video conferencing is becoming increasingly widely used as a medium for group communication. It has the same advantages as conference calling with regard to travel time and for those people who need communications with groups in different parts of the world or who need several diverse meetings in one day.

Live Meeting

There are many proprietary and DIY conferencing set-ups available, as well as some interesting alternatives, such as Live Meeting, which is a hosted, real time Web conferencing service. It enables participants to communicate and collaborate with anyone, anywhere – using a PC and an Internet connection. It is an interesting tool. More information can be found at www.office.microsoft.com

If you use any communication that allows visual contact, it is worthwhile thinking not only about good meetings practice, but also about how you present to camera. Although the technologies allow people to meet 'face to face', none allow participants to use all of their verbal and non-verbal skills as fully as they would in a real time, face-to-face conversation. Participants should be aware that, as a result, any vocal or visual signals they give out are potentially open to greater misunderstanding than would usually be the case.

Instant Messaging

Increasingly, many people use Instant Messaging whilst simultaneously participating in a conference call or during a meeting that they are attending in person. Current reports suggest that this is often being used in a subversive way, to have a secondary conversation – about other participants, the meeting content or even to lobby for an outcome that a sub-group are seeking to achieve.

It is important to understand that these parallel meetings **do** take place – even if you are not currently party to them. In traditional meetings, the best way to deal with the challenge is for the chairperson to ask at the beginning of any event to have PC lids down and all phones switched off.

It is imperative that parallel meetings should not be allowed and, as in all other aspects of business, the leader's ability to model good behaviour and set an appropriate example is key!

Chapter 8

Email Guidelines

- The challenge of email
- Email flow
- Reviewing the Inbox - inputs
- Email usage
- Turn off the incoming mail alert
- Organising email
- Reducing the flow of email
- Is email the right tool?
- Responding to email
- The 4 D's and the PASS Model
- Automatic signature
- To set an OOM
- Good practice
- Writing a good email
- Email on the move
- Shared access to email
- Saving corporate time
- Using other tools
- Action plan for change

The challenge of email

The use of email has revolutionised communications by increasing the ease and speed at which individuals and organisations can interact with each other – but poor discipline, bad practices and a lack of agreed conventions for its use have come to outweigh the undoubted benefits – to the extent that email is now recognised as being one of the main causes of work related stress and is amongst the top 10 causes of stress in general.

People may feel that email puts them under pressure for different reasons. These may be as diverse as:

- **concern by individuals about their own technical shortcomings.**
- **the weight of being constantly available and having an ever filling Inbox, with no apparent 'off tap' or means of slowing the flow down.**
- **living in a 'do, do, do' culture.**
- **feeling the need to work longer hours to keep up with email volumes.**

Above all, emails are time-consuming. They eat up an ever-increasing chunk of our working days, and they are changing our working practices.

In 2003 UK Department of Trade and Industry figures estimated that people were spending an average of 49 minutes per day working with emails – limited observation will confirm to the rest of us that as each year passes, these figures must be growing exponentially!

It is now common for people to spend several hours each day working through email, sometimes before they start the formal 'working day' and again before they feel able to close down at the end of the day.

Some users check their email twenty or more times during the course of the day, with usage in general peaking late afternoon and early evening. For many, email has become the principle medium for receiving, progressing and delivering tasks in their day-to-day job – whether that is what their job description says they should be doing, or not. Some jobs demand that email access is on tap. Others allow discretion and choice. Which is the case for you?

The combination of increasing volumes of email (much of it hard to prioritise), and the perceived pressure to respond immediately to ALL incoming emails, mean that far from being a 'productivity tool', email has all too often become a 'productivity detractor'.

Levels of effectiveness are such that an average user might waste up to 25 days per year, with the extreme user wasting as much as 55 potentially productive days per year.

Before you get caught up in processing email, look at the opportunity cost. What other aspects of your job is the time that you spend on email preventing you from engaging with?

What is your attitude to email? Do you find that you need and enjoy an 'email fix'?

___

___

___

How long do you think you spend on email each day?

___

___

___

How many emails do you think you send and receive?

___

___

___

Most people tend to overestimate their email usage – but in truth it is not just the *quantity* of emails, but also the *quality* and speed of transacting that is worthy of attention. Use the Email flow analysis chart (Figure 37) to record your actual email flow.

Email flow **Email flow analysis chart**

- ❑ Keep a record over a number of days – a whole working week should provide some really good data. Use one chart per day.
- ❑ Record the open and closing time whenever you access your email and keep a running total of cumulative time spent dealing with mails.
- ❑ Make a note of the quantities of emails both received and sent.

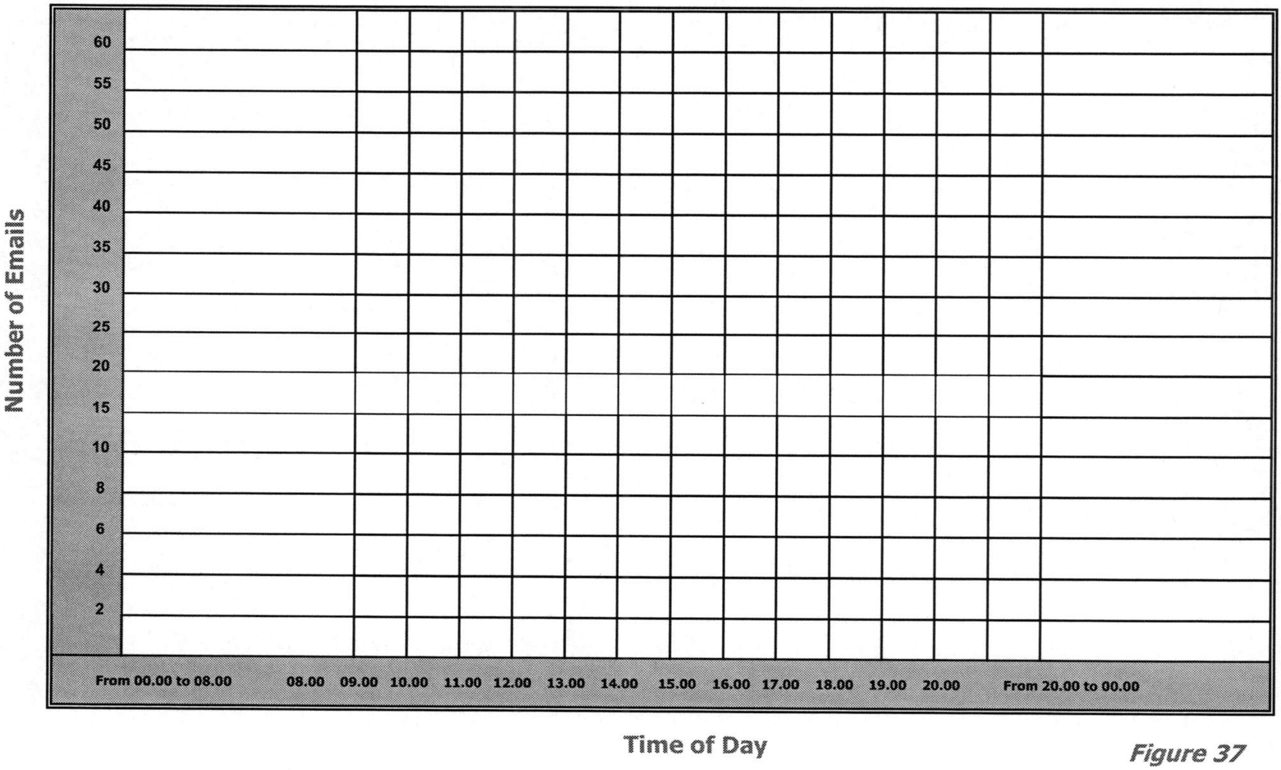

Number of Emails														
60														
55														
50														
45														
40														
35														
30														
25														
20														
15														
10														
8														
6														
4														
2														
	From 00.00 to 08.00	08.00	09.00	10.00	11.00	12.00	13.00	14.00	15.00	16.00	17.00	18.00	19.00	20.00	From 20.00 to 00.00

Time of Day

Figure 37

Reviewing the Inbox – inputs

Having completed your research:

What was the actual (cumulative) time you spent dealing with email on a daily and a weekly basis?

____

____

____

How many separate visits did you access your email inbox on a daily or weekly basis?

____

____

____

How many incoming emails did you receive?

____

____

____

How many outgoing emails did you send?

____

____

____

When were your times of peak activity?

____

____

____

Which emails annoyed you or made you feel stressed? What is it about them that particularly concern or irritates you?

____

____

____

What is the ratio of useful emails to junk or comparatively low value emails?

What conclusions can you draw from this?

What is your action plan now?

By adopting some simple email guidelines, it is possible to leverage great benefits, both for yourself and the people that you interact with. Be prepared to raise email usage as an issue worthy of review and to take responsibility for leading improvement.

Email usage

There are a number of things that will influence email usage:

- ❑ **Your function.**
- ❑ **Your internal lines of reporting.**
- ❑ **The nature of your task load.**
- ❑ **Your market sector.**
- ❑ **Your need for, and use of, information.**
- ❑ **Your range of contacts and networks.**
- ❑ **The size of your organisation.**
- ❑ **The number of people you need to keep simultaneously informed.**
- ❑ **Your need for international communication.**
- ❑ **Personal preferences.**

Whatever your needs for email communication inwards and outwards, it is vital to control the amount of time it consumes, and always to be aware of the difference between 'information' and 'noise'.

Information can be described as emails that add value to you and which fit in with your style and approach.

Excess 'noise' can be described as those emails you receive which are of little or no importance to you, that you would normally look at quickly or skip over. You may bin them immediately, or just as likely, they may sink to the bottom of your Inbox unsorted or unread because you cannot decide where to file them or what to do with them!

❑ **Noise includes:**

- junk mail, e-newsletters, circulars.
- contacts from old customers and suppliers; unsolicited approaches or referrals from prospective customers and suppliers.
- contacts from colleagues, Cc'd information, jokes and any other outdated, unwanted or unrequested emails.

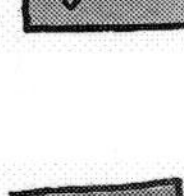

Review the flow of your Inbox regularly. Separate the content that you need from the content that you do not. Decide what needs to be stored, what needs to be actioned, and what can be deleted.

Look again at your data gleaned from completing the email flow analysis chart.

Who do you have most email correspondence with?

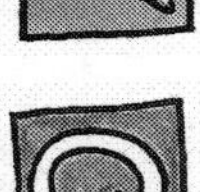

____

____

____

What proportion of your received mail is information and what proportion is noise?

____

____

____

What can you do to adjust the information/noise ratio?

____

____

____

Manage your time by limiting the number of times you check for incoming mail. Cut the number of visits to your Inbox gradually – email is addictive and it is pointless trying to cut down from 20 visits to 4 visits at a stroke!

Fight the need to be online all the time

Have you ever been caught out because you did not respond to an email immediately? Very few people honestly have. If they have, it is often because they failed to respond to a request from someone who had exceptionally short timescales.

Your fault or theirs?

In the unusual case where there is a problem because of delayed response to an 'urgent' email, ask yourself the following questions:

- ❑ Was the problem with you or with the sender?
- ❑ Was it reasonable to classify this particular request as urgent, or was it just the result of bad planning on their part?
- ❑ Does your job role require that you should monitor your email (to the exclusion of anything else) every minute of the day, or do you have other things to do?
- ❑ Might the sender have communicated their request sooner?
- ❑ Might the sender have chosen a different means of communication – for example by telephone or face-to face conversation?

Email is not the best tool for communication that requires an immediate response – much better to use the phone or even to send an SMS message.

Turn off the incoming mail alert

Do not allow your attention to be caught by an incoming message. Hear the 'ping' and you may be tempted to think that the new mail is urgent, important or even just plain interesting (just like every letter contains a cheque!), but more possibly, it is not!

The email and the email 'ping' is an interrupter – treat it as such; it can wait until **you** are ready to view your Inbox.

Turn off the audible message alert – do not allow your Inbox to entice you away from the things that you need to do!

From the **Tools** option in the headings select **Options**. Once in Options select **E-mail options**. Click **OK**. Then select **Advanced E-mail Options**. Click **OK**.

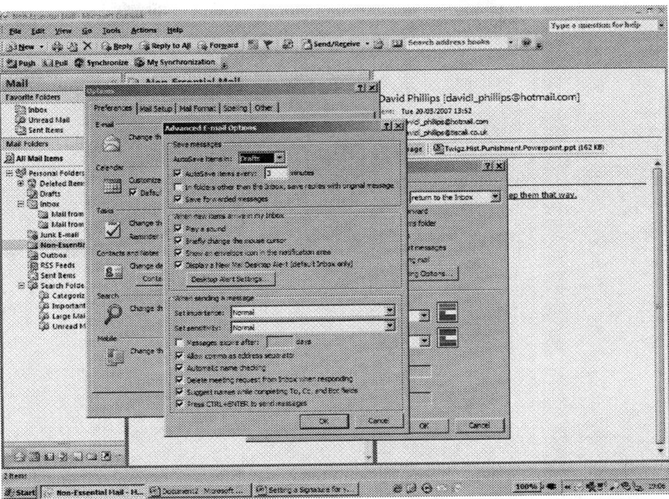

Figure 38

In the **Advanced E-mail Options** click to un-tick the **Play a sound** option in the second block down. Click **OK**.

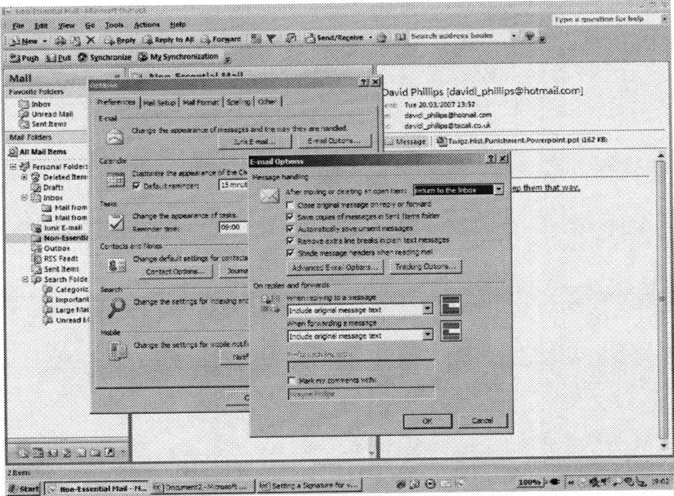

Figure 39

Remember: It is up to you to decide when you want to be interrupted!

Organising email

❑ **There are many things that you can do to save time organising emails.** These include:

- Clearing your Inbox regularly.
- Creating short-cuts from your email to key applications and files that you use frequently.

- ❑ **Filter your email** – sort material from different sources or on different subjects into folders in your email database, to help manage the size of your Inbox.
- ❑ **Create rules to automatically filter non-essential email.**

To set rules you need to be using a non-web based email client, (e.g. tiscali.co.uk). http:// web emails such as hotmail will not work for creating rules.

From **Tools** select **Rules and Alerts**.

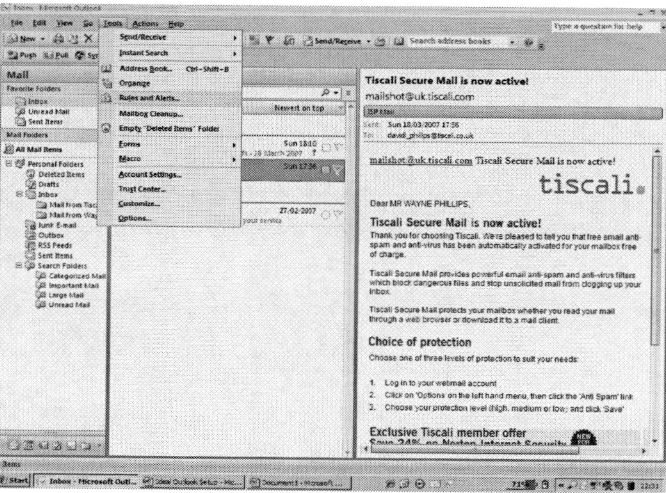

Figure 40

Once in the rules section, select **New Rule**, then select the Rule that suits you best.

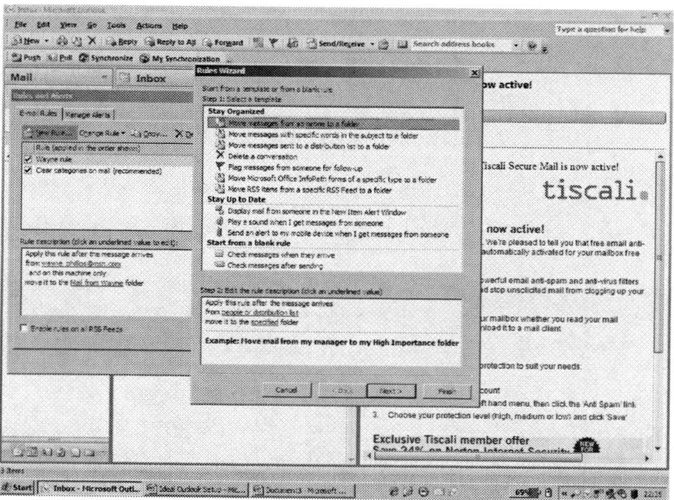

Figure 41

For this example we will use the top rule, **Move message from someone to a folder**. Once this is selected click **Next**. This will take you on to a page where you can define your rule in greater detail. To minimise non-essential mail it would be a good idea to check the following boxes...

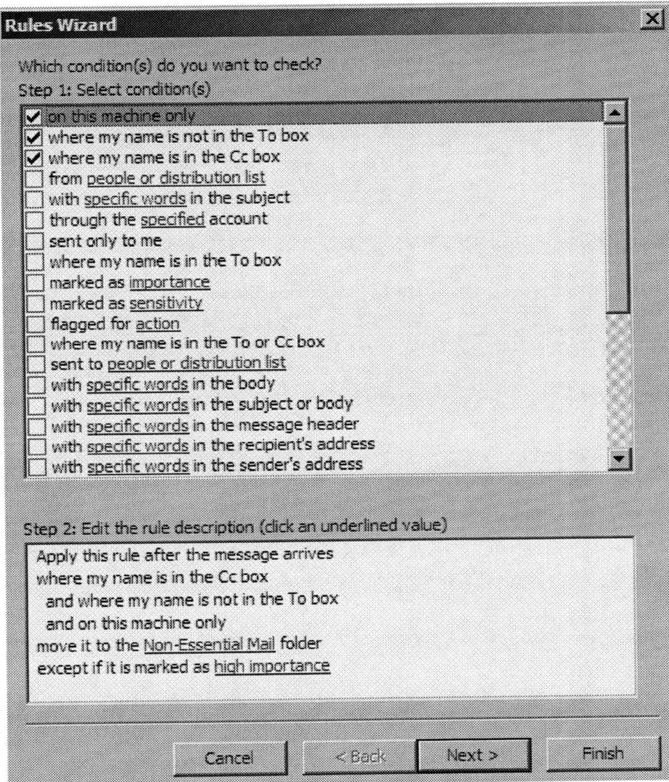

Figure 42

This means that you now only get emails that are sent directly to you in the **To...** box, and not ones in which you are Cc'd onto.

Why not mail your entire contacts list, explaining that due to the number of emails that you receive, you will no longer commit to reading or responding to mails where you are on the Cc... line? The message is clear. If it is important please send it to me – otherwise please do not bother!!

Next, click on the underlined **specified** and create a new non-essential mail folder. This folder will appear on the left hand side in the folders column.

After doing this there is another screen where you can set exceptions to the rules and one good option to check here would be **except if it is marked as high importance**.

For some people, implementing this idea alone will reduce traffic into their inbox by as much as 25%!

Follow the last few self-help steps and you now have a rule that differentiates the important email from the less important.

- ❑ **Try a list digest** – if you are on a mailing list and find the traffic overwhelming, see if there is a 'digest' version that allows you to get a single large message with the day's posts, instead of countless individual emails throughout the day – this can really help to cut down on 'noise' and clutter.
- ❑ **Use templates for frequently used responses** – such as directions to your office. Create it once and use it time after time.
- ❑ **Use folders to store both sent and received mails.**
- ❑ **Store received mails in folders that reflect your core areas of responsibility** – **Clients**, **Customers**, **Projects** and so on, that each hold more specific sub-folders (**Clients** – Client A, Client B, Client C; **Customers** – Customer A, Customer B, Customer C; **Projects** – Project A, Project B, Project C and so on).
- ❑ **Do not attempt to file sent mails in the same way, as this can be time consuming** – instead store them in Quarterly files: **2007 Q3**, **2007 Q4**, **2008 Q1** and so on.
- ❑ **Do not save mails that are no longer required** – edit as you file.

These good housekeeping ideas will give you structure and empty both your sent and deleted boxes – preventing you from having any 'Inbox full' messages from your Administrator.

Customise your Outlook view

There are many ways to do this. The key is not to accept the standard way, but instead to think through and then create the best format for you. For example:

- Folders list (at left)
- Main Screen (middle)
- Task pad (bottom right)

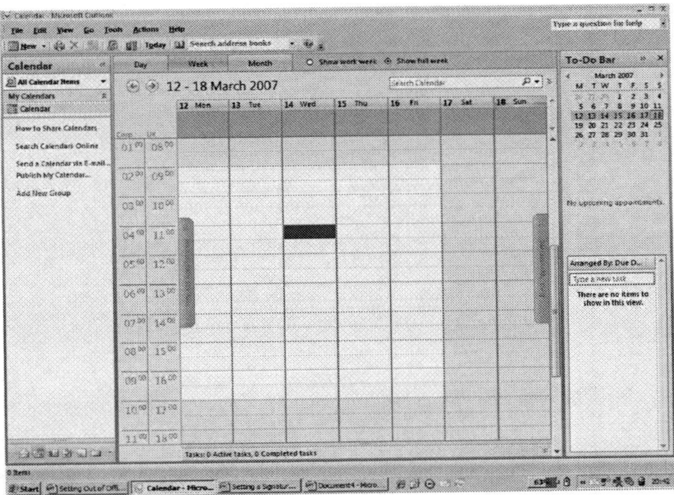

Figure 43

- **Changing the setup to calendar**

If you do not like having the **To-Do Bar** and just prefer having a larger calendar view, go to **View** in the headings column. Click on **To-Do Bar** and select **minimize** or **off**.

To switch between the **Calendar** and **E-mail**, use the small picture icons in the bottom left hand corner in the **Folders** pane.

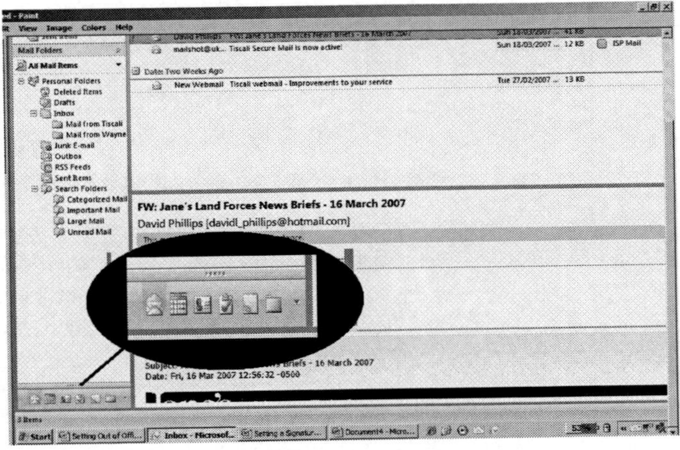

Figure 44

In the **E-mail** pane you can also remove the **To-Do Bar** (situated on the extreme right margin above), in the same way as in calendar mode.

If you wish to do so, you can rearrange the viewing pane by going into **View** and then clicking on the **Reading Pane** option.

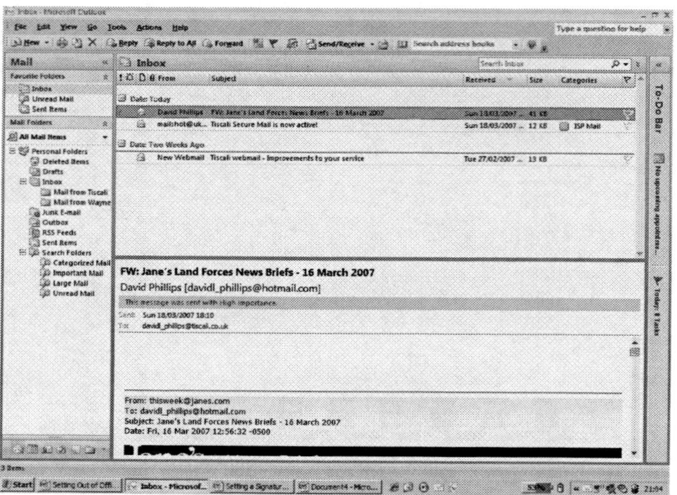

Figure 45

Reducing the flow of email

❑ **There are many things that you can do to reduce the flow of emails:**

- Prioritise information – restrict the number of sources of information that you access, to those that are essential to doing your job.
- Talk, rather than using email as your default.
- Cut down on ping-pong – after 4 or 5 mails, pick up the phone!
- P–a–u–s–e before replying. If a reply is not needed, do not send one.
- Do not mail to say 'thank you' for a job or task that you would expect someone to do – if their service to you has been extraordinary then a call, a face-to-face or a letter may be more appropriate anyway.
- Consider finishing your mail with the words 'No reply needed', to end correspondence on this subject.

❑ **Put an end to unwanted mail and watch out for:**

- People who are playing a political game.
- People who are in the business of 'covering their backside'.
- Old projects (in which you are no longer involved).
- Newsletters and circulars that used to have appeal, but which are no longer relevant.
- Mails relating to a previous job or responsibilities.

Always ask yourself why have I been sent this mail?

- ❑ **Do not just delete unwanted mails, but return them with a polite explanation of why you no longer need it.** This may be hard to do initially, but if you can bite the bullet once, it will save time thereafter.
- ❑ **Quick ways to remove irrelevant mails:**
  - Apply the 'email by exception' rule – (Let people know: "I trust you – please get on with it – just include me if I need to know anything, and of course do not give me any scary surprises!")
  - Unsubscribe to unwanted newsletters – do not be tempted to introduce other people without their permission. This is akin to joining them to book or wine clubs which you think are great, but have no relevance to them.
  - Inform your IT administrator about unwanted junk mail.
  - Develop and encourage the use of shared information areas.

Is email the right tool?

There will be many occasions where email is not the best tool and person-to-person conversation would be preferable, but there is a real time management dilemma here. Phoning somebody or walking to their desk suggests that this is a great time for you to make the interruption. If you choose not to email, but to phone or visit instead, save up your interruptions for one hit, at a time that suits both you and the recipient.

For many well-disciplined people, having other people sending them emails, which they open when they are ready to be disturbed, is actually quite a good time management device. So we need some balance here. Use email when appropriate, and phone or visit when appropriate; consider the time management implications of your choice for both parties.

In other words, use a mixture of communication tools and choose the most appropriate for each occasion.

It is not appropriate to communicate by email when dealing with:

- ❑ Matters to do with someone's individual relationship with the business.
- ❑ Complex issues.
- ❑ Personal issues or issues of a delicate nature.

Neither is it appropriate to communicate by email on any occasion when it would be beneficial to read another person's body language or to be able to display emotion (compassion, empathy, understanding) oneself.

Responding to email

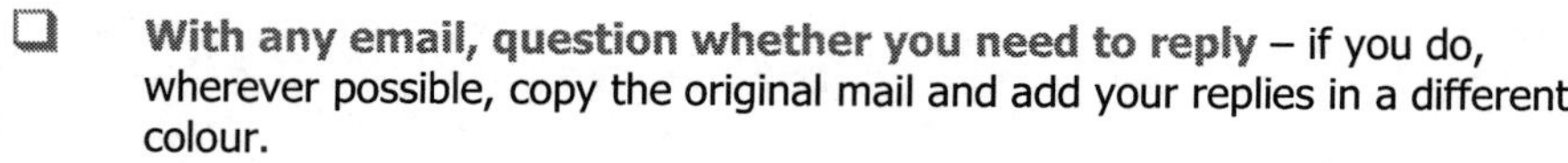

- ❑ **With any email, question whether you need to reply** – if you do, wherever possible, copy the original mail and add your replies in a different colour.
- ❑ **Keep addressees to a minimum –** think carefully before hitting **Reply All** – do you want to share your database with everyone?

When sending email, some people place all of the email aliases into the **To...** field.

There are two drawbacks to this:

1. All recipients know that you have sent the same message to many other email addresses, which they now have access to.
2. You are publishing someone else's email alias without their permission.

To avoid this, place all addressees in the **Bcc...** field (Blind carbon copy) and address the mail **To...** yourself.

You could include the mailing list email address in the **To...** field, or even better, if you have Microsoft Outlook and Word you can do a mail merge and create one message for each recipient.

For more information on how to do a Word mail merge, consult the Help in Word or visit:

http://office.microsoft.com/en-gb/training.

Only use **Reply to All i**f you really need your message to be seen by each person who received the original message. If not, just press **Reply**.

Do not Reply, Cc... or Bcc... the World.

- ❑ **The purpose of the Cc... line is to provide a courtesy copy** – it needs to be read or filed and have no action taken.

If you consistently copy in the world, you will devalue your own communication and recipients are less likely to discover or read an important communication amongst all the other stuff.

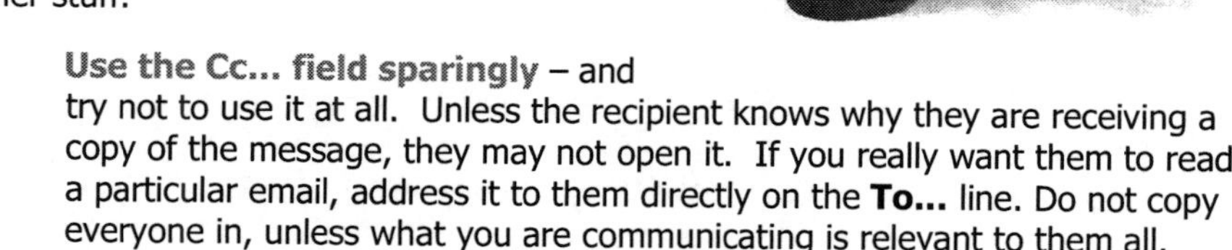

- ❑ **Use the Cc... field sparingly** – and try not to use it at all. Unless the recipient knows why they are receiving a copy of the message, they may not open it. If you really want them to read a particular email, address it to them directly on the **To...** line. Do not copy everyone in, unless what you are communicating is relevant to them all.

- ❑ **Consider using a share point for group information or send links as part of a smaller email**, so that individuals can access the information if and when they want to.
- ❑ **The purpose of the Bcc... line is to protect the integrity of your distribution list** and to prevent the main recipient from seeing who else has received a reply.
- ❑ **Be careful with Bcc...** – why would you want to send a copy of an email that has been sent to a third party, without the original recipient knowing that you have done it?

BCC... can be seen as being rather sneaky and the only really acceptable use for it is as a way of hiding or protecting your Sent To... list from other recipients.

- ❑ **Never assume that email is private or confidential** – as with all technology, things can go array.
  - With some email systems, the email administrator has the ability to read any and all email messages.
  - Some companies monitor employees' email to ensure users are not wasting time on frivolous messages, or leaking company secrets.
- ❑ **Be aware – if you sent it from the office, it came from the office** – personal emails sent in office time, using a company email alias can be taken to be official communication, so beware of what you send!

The Decision Cycle – There are 3 fundamental questions that will help you to process email.

- ❑ **Question 1: What is this?**
  - There can be a temptation to open an email, find that it is not very interesting and close it again
  - Once an email is open, never close it without taking action.
- ❑ **Question 2: How is this actionable?**
  - Think about the email.
  - Ask does this relate to my objectives?
  - Do I need to do this?
  - Could somebody else do it?
- ❑ **Question 3: What is the next action?**
  - What is the next physical, 'doable' step?

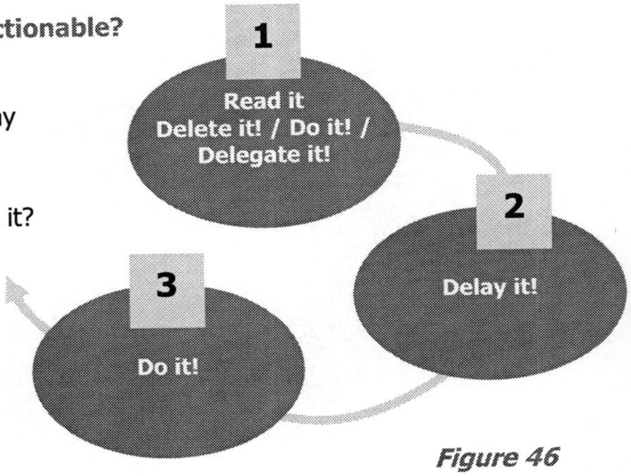

Figure 46

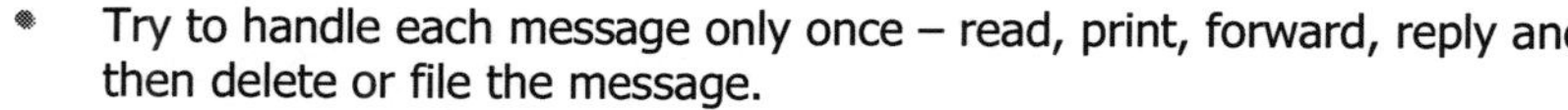

- Try to handle each message only once – read, print, forward, reply and then delete or file the message.
- If you need to invite Muna, Christof and Liv to a meeting, then take that one-step action immediately.

The 4 D's and the PASS Model

Apply the 4 D's (Delete it! Do it! Delegate it! Delay it!), as shown in the Decision Cycle above, to help you to distinguish the 'information' from the 'noise':

- ❑ **Delete it!** If a mail is not actionable and you do not need it for reference – it is noise, so dump it! The delete button is your greatest ally in overcoming wasted time and effort.
- ❑ **Do it!** If you are going to respond to a mail – do it, be proactive! Focus on speed and volume.

Look at each email, identify potentially quick replies (those that take less than 2 minutes to process) and deal with them immediately. Using this method, you can process up to 60 emails an hour and clear the bulk of your Inbox very quickly. Email that takes longer than 2 minutes to deal with, or that demand more careful thought, can be filed in your task folder and again, time should be set aside in the day to clear this.

Really stretch yourself to deal with emails once and take pleasure in clearing as many from the Inbox as you can in less than 2 minutes each.

- ❑ **Delegate it!** As with everything else in business, if you can delegate, do so.
  - Explain what you need and when you need it.
  - If you want to follow-up on what you have delegated, copy yourself on the **Cc...** line of the email. (Notwithstanding the changes recommended to Cc'd mail earlier.) When you receive the copy, you can track it by creating a Waiting category on your task list.
- ❑ **Delay it!** If it takes longer than 2 minutes, simply defer it to your task list, as outlined above. Re-label the subject line with the next action and store it in the appropriate category. Set aside time to deal with those more demanding or time-consuming emails.

This process may not feel natural, but it is worthwhile changing your behaviour from reactive to proactive because of the time you will save and the stress you will avoid.

- ❑ **Good practice for sending emails** – to manage email effectively, you must be results-oriented, which means having:
  - identified clear goals and objectives.
  - identified which tasks to work on to reach those goals and objectives.
  - ... and then you must plan to, and actually spend, time on those tasks, otherwise, how can you prioritise?
- ❑ **When sending email, use the email PASS model** (based on the work of Sally McGhee). Ask yourself:
  - What is the **PURPOSE** of my email – does it link to an objective?
  - What **ACTION** is involved – does it have a due date?
  - What **SUPPORTING** documentation do I need to include?
  - Have I summarised my communication in the **SUBJECT** line?
- ❑ **PURPOSE**
  - Apply the 4 D's. Ask: Does this email relate to one of your objectives?
  - If not, renegotiate it or disengage from it.
  - If it is relevant, ask: What do I want to achieve by sending this email?
- ❑ **ACTION**
  - Is any action required by you or the recipient, or is this mail for information only?
  - What are the deadline dates?
- ❑ **SUPPORT documentation**:
  - What supporting information will the recipient require? (Getting this right will reduce the need for them to come back to you with supplementary questions, or with requests for more information.)
- ❑ **Summarise on the SUBJECT line**. For example:

  'Step System integration project. Create a monthly report on SharePoint, beginning 05.07.07'

  This will help the recipient to:
  - prioritise, organise and process their emails efficiently.
  - know what the email relates to, so that they can file and find it again.
  - know what their responsibility is and when it is due.
  - use their own password protected accounts.
- ❑ **Link time critical emails to your calendar or task list** so you can track them and they will be flagged up when necessary.

❑ **Create an automatic signature** – to put your pre-defined text at the bottom of every email. This would normally include:

- your name and job title.
- company name, email address, web and telephone contact details and perhaps your company address and current marketing strap line.

Automatic signature

Save time on every email by using an automatic signature. To set this up, open **Tools** from the headings column and click on **Options** at the bottom of the list. Select **Mail Format** and then open the **Signatures** tab, about two-thirds down the page.

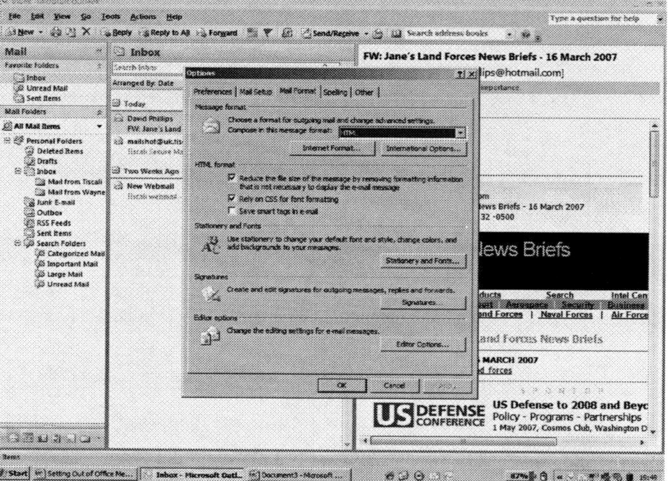

Figure 47

Select **New** and then follow the directions to enter your details. Click **OK** and your signature will be added to the bottom of your emails.

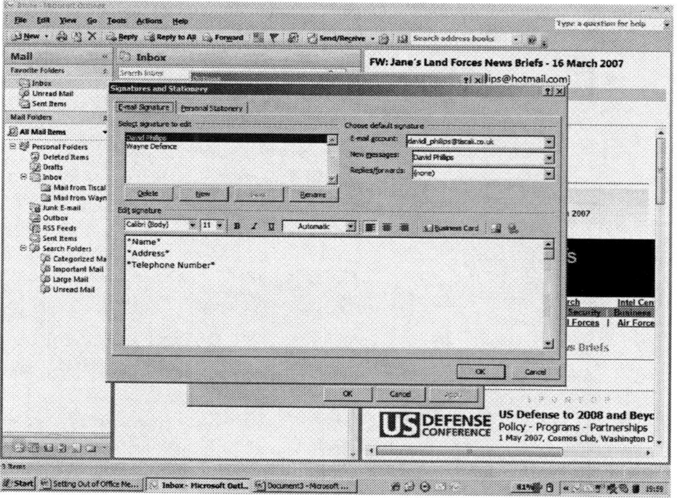

Figure 48

To speed up the process of sending mails to distinct groups, use distribution lists (group lists) and make sure that they are up-to-date.

Open the **File** menu, click **New**, and then click **Distribution List**.

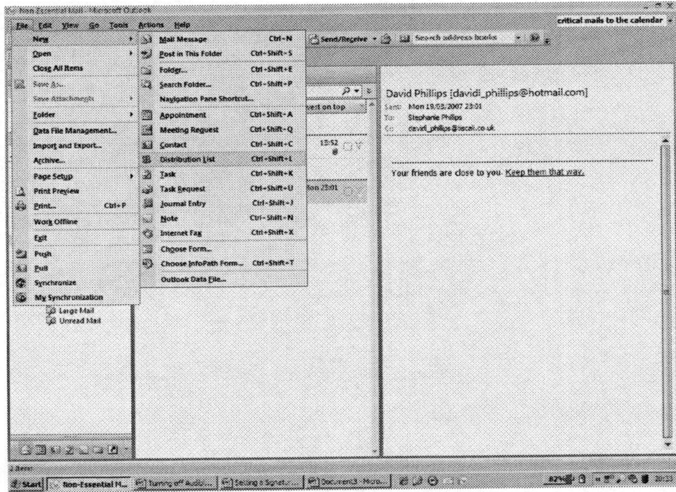

Figure 49

In the **Name** box, type a name. On the **Distribution List** tab, click **Select Members**. In the **Members** tab click **Add New** and type in their email address.

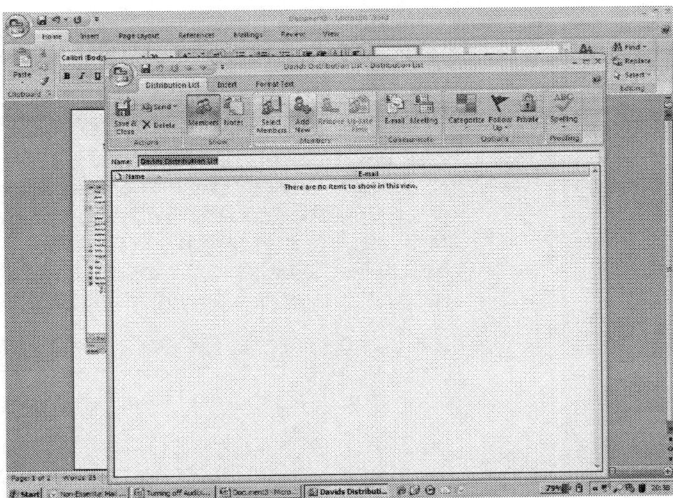

Figure 50

Repeat as necessary until you have all the contacts you want in the group. To use your distribution list, go to **Send E-Mail**, click on the **To...** button and select **Use Distribution List**.

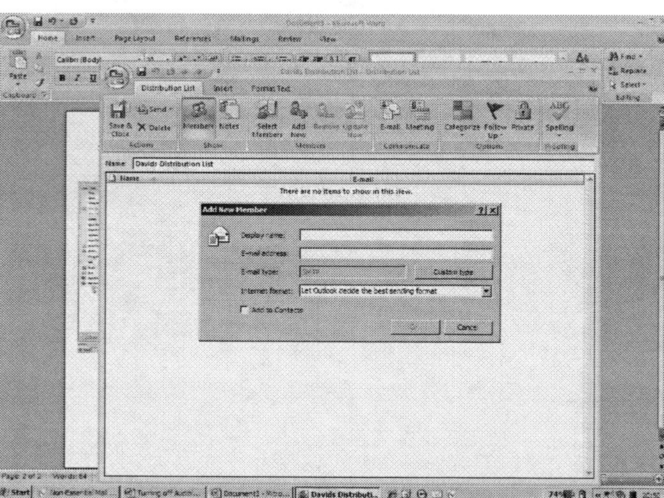

Figure 51

Communication has changed. Many people entering business today may never have written a formal or business letter. Their main form of correspondence hitherto is likely to have been electronic and they are unwitting champions of the transition from formal and evenly paced communication, to a style that is much more immediate, fast and fluid.

Good practice

- ❑ **Make your email communication accurate** – email correspondence should be clear. When you respond to others ensure that you answer all questions, pre-empting the need for any further questions.

- ❑ **Edit emotion out of your reply** – and deal with difficult or contentious issues face-to-face. Failing to do this will lead to frustration, unnecessary email ping-pong and the likelihood of a 'Flame' response. A flame is a response to a mail, which you may have sent to 20 people, but which has been taken to be abrupt, rude, pernickety (add your own words here) by one recipient and, as a result, they have fired off a heated response.

  It is very tempting to get into a 'flame war', but try to be sensitive and conciliatory, try to see the email from the other person's point of view, think through your response and even when you have written it, p-a-u-s-e before you send.

  Ask yourself, will my reply help the situation or make it worse? Do I want to (can I afford to) end communication or sour relations with this individual for ever?

It is important to focus on adult to adult conversation and to draw flame conversations to an end as soon as possible.

- ❑ **If a rapid response is required by the sender** – then communicating earlier, having a face-to-face conversation or using the telephone may be a more appropriate and less stressful option.
- ❑ **Answer emails with a response time** – decide on your personal or departmental response time quality standard. Either reply within it, or send a holding mail saying that you are in receipt of their communication and that you will get back to them by a specified time and date. This will put the correspondent's mind at rest, help them to manage their stress and encourage them to be patient.
- ❑ **Do not respond too quickly** – if you respond to mail as soon as you receive it, you may find yourself entering into a virtually 'live' dialogue, at the expense of other work. It is acceptable to access your emails 2 or 3 times a day. Use an OOM (see below) to manage expectations. Do not allow the excitement of email to disturb or distract you from other priorities.

It may be the case however that the email content is complicated and the parties involved may require a record, making email a preferred medium. A more appropriate personal quality standard might be to make a commitment with oneself to respond to each mail within at least 24 hours, and preferably within the same working day.

- ❑ **Do not respond to emails when you are on leave** – in the days before email, did you ask for your paper intray to be forwarded to you? Leave a well-structured Out of Office Message (OOM) instead.
- ❑ **Out of Office Message (OOM)** – is an automated response to incoming mails. You can still read and respond to mails when the OOM is switched on, should you wish to do so.

To set an OOM

Select **Tools** – if **Out of Office Assistant** is available it will be in the drop down menu. Click to open and then select **Send Out of Office auto-replies**. Type in the message you want to have sent out and click **OK**.

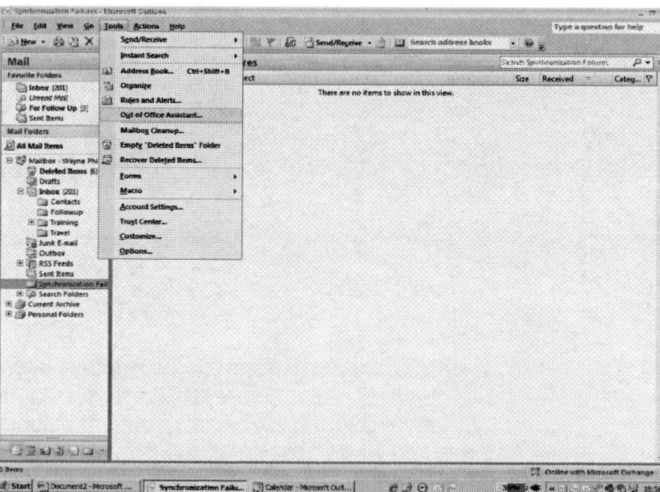

Figure 52

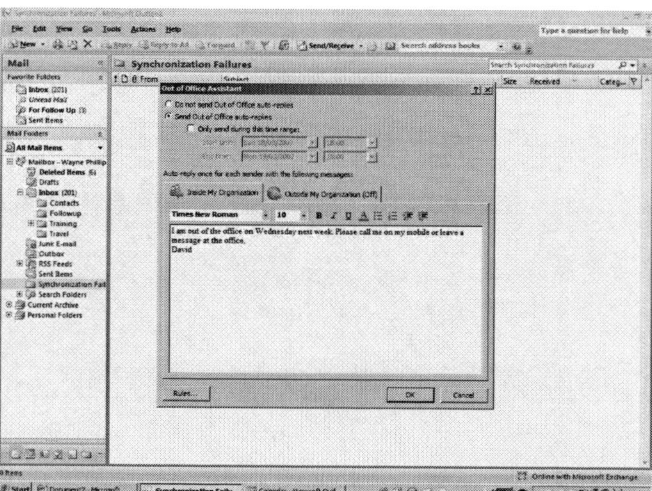

Figure 53

Using an OOM will help people to understand that you will not be responding immediately and will also have the benefit of telling them when you **will** be able to respond and what alternative action they can take if they have an emergency.

Make your OOM succinct, containing one alternative contact address and telephone number.

- ❑ **Do not respond to emails if you have other pressing work to do** – if you would prefer not to be disturbed – say so! It is perfectly acceptable to have an OOM set for half a day, while you attend meetings or work on other priorities.

Using OOM's will help you to manage others' expectations and encourage them to understand that you are not a slave to email. It encourages them to use alternative means of communication, if they have something urgent to transmit and will significantly reduce the number of mails collecting in your Inbox whilst you are out of email contact.

- ❑ **Manage the size of your attachments** – although Broadband has helped to ease the transmission of large attachments, there will be no guarantee that just because you can send it, the recipient will be able to receive it.

  Segment large files, zip them up or use a CD or a Memory Stick. It is good manners to alert a recipient if you are intending to send a particularly large file.

- ❑ **Do not attach unnecessary files** – and compress those that you do send. Establish rules for handling confidential or copyright information. Ensure that everyone understands the potential contractual significance of emails and the legal responsibilities that they entail.

- ❑ **Use a spellchecker** – and check that your emails are addressed to the right recipients and that they say exactly what you want them to say.

- ❑ **Read your 'finished' emails before you send them** – imagine yourself as the recipient and check for style, tone, meaning, grammar and spellings. This will help to ensure that your mails are clear, professional and unambiguous.

- ❑ **Add disclaimers to your emails** – as in all other areas, it is important to comply with legal and your own company's regulations and norms. Including disclaimers as a default footer to your email will help to protect both you and your company from any liability.

For example:

"This email is confidential and is intended for the use of the named recipient only. If you have received this mail in error, please inform us immediately and then delete it. Unless it specifically states otherwise, this email does not form part of a contract."

Company law in the UK also makes it necessary to list your company's registration number, place of registration and registered office address on both your website and on email footers.

Writing a good email

When writing emails keep them short and to the point. Here are some tips which will help to save time and improve productivity in email communication:

- ❑ **Think of emails as being like any other sort of communication** – they need to be immediately accessible to the recipients.
- ❑ **Make the subject headings meaningful.**
- ❑ **Choose the appropriate greeting and use the person's name.**
- ❑ **Avoid using emoticons, diverse fonts, colours, backgrounds.**
- ❑ **Write the email from the reader's point of view.** Break it up into short paragraphs, with bold subtitles. Limit the content of mail to one page.
- ❑ **Make sure that the email has a clear beginning, middle and end.**
- ❑ **Keep them concise** – short, sharp, to the point and avoid using capitals in the main text.
- ❑ **Set your email out in an inverted triangle, as used in newspaper articles.** Give the message purpose at the start, in the headline and then progress or develop your point through the body of the email. In other words, begin with the punch line and then develop your message or argument accordingly.
- ❑ **For multiple questions, consider using more than one mail.**
- ❑ **Consider copying the other person's mail if it needs a reply and adding your comments in a different colour** – topping and tailing the mail with a one sentence explanation.
- ❑ **Make sure that your mail has all the necessary information, attachments and links** to avoid the need for the recipient to request supplementary information.
- ❑ **Limit the use of attachments** – investigate the use of bulletin boards to pass on a lot of information, or to inform whole groups.

- ❑ **Use SharePoint or other portals to store information that several people will need to access** – do not send files, send links.
- ❑ **Mark the 'subject' line carefully** – only label email with 'URGENT', if it really is urgent and 'CONFIDENTIAL', if it really is confidential.
- ❑ **Only email those people who need your information.** Do not automatically press the **Reply** or **Reply to all** buttons, or use outdated group mailing lists.
- ❑ **P-a-u-s-e before you send.**
- ❑ **Speak before you email anything complex** – try the phone, or arrange a meeting if it is more appropriate.
- ❑ **And finally...** as part of good practice: Introduce a weekly housekeeping review and tidy up your email usage.

Email on the move

Being able to email on the move has many benefits – it means that you can:

- ❑ **feel in control.**
- ❑ **stay in touch and be responsive to the needs of others.**
- ❑ **keep on top of your Inbox** – there is no backlog building up.
- ❑ **be able to micromanage *and* keep your communications immediate** – making you feel 'in the swim'.

Disadvantages:

The drawbacks to emailing on the move include the following:

- ❑ **it speeds up the process of working** – speeds up the pace and immediacy of decision-making, which may not suit everybody's natural style.
- ❑ **it is an activity that prevents you from doing other things** – thinking, reading, communicating face-to-face.
- ❑ **it means that you always have to carry hand held tools or a PC.**
- ❑ **it is a security risk.**
- ❑ **you are never quite switching off.**

Going off-line occasionally and being disciplined in the use of email will have a significant impact on your ability to achieve work / life balance. Whilst you may be happy to always 'stay in touch', your partner, family and friends may be less enamoured of the situation!

You really do have a choice – the crunch is really based around the volume of urgent mail that you honestly receive. If a high proportion of the mail you receive requires a quick or immediate response, and if your part of the business cannot function without you doing so, then you probably do need to have access on the move. However, do not feel guilty if you choose not to have access to additional tools, whilst on the move. Always consider the opportunity cost of any decision.

Ask yourself:

How do I currently use my time away from my desk and how important is it that I continue to do these things?

____

____

____

If I spend my time on emails instead, when will I do these other things?

____

____

____

Whatever choice you make, it must be one that adds value to the quality or quantity of work that you can manage.

Shared access to email

Many bosses and PAs face a dilemma over who should manage the email – this is possibly also an issue in small businesses or partnerships, where there is shared management.

There are really only three options for a boss and PA to choose from:

1. The PA keeps a firm hand on the controls and behaves like a traditional gatekeeper.
2. The Boss and PA both have access.
3. The Boss runs his or her own Inbox, with occasional support.

Begin by getting clarity:

- ❑ **Choose your preferred option from 1, 2 or 3 above.**
- ❑ **Agree who will deal with what and establish time parameters** – frequency, speed of reply, and so on.
- ❑ **Agree on a folder structure which is user-friendly and logical to both parties.** Perhaps base this on key areas of responsibility already established and on existing menus used for filing information in Word.
- ❑ **Always mark as unread any emails you have skimmed, but which have not been completely dealt with.**
- ❑ **Ensure emails are only handled once by each person.**
- ❑ **Decide where (and on whose PC) it will be best to store the old emails.**
- ❑ **Review and revise folder names over time** – they will change as the job develops and as projects, tasks and business relationships come in and out of play.
- ❑ **Stick to the agreed processes.**

Saving corporate time

Many of the ideas listed in this chapter are applicable to individuals, teams and the wider business. If your corporate email policy is under-developed, you can help by contributing to the creation of one for your business – if there is one already, check it out and offer your ideas for proactive improvement.

Using other tools

If you are thinking of using or updating your use of technology away from the office (Laptop, Tablet, PDAs, Smart phones) be aware that there will always be a trade-off between functionality and size. There are no shortages of options available (each displaying diverse features and benefits) and these are being constantly revised and up-dated.

Action plan for change

Many people are looking for 'the Holy Grail', the one size fits all solution, which may not currently exist and which is purely subjective anyway. There is no doubt however that utilising technology on the move, being able to synchronise diaries and appointments, as well as accessing the company server and the internet can all lead to greatly enhanced effectiveness.

For all its shortcomings, email will continue to be a highly valued business tool – the important thing is to exercise discretion and good practice in your own use.

From the list below, select your biggest email stressors? What proactive actions can you take to deal with them?

____

____

____

1.	**Feeling pressured by volume of emails**
2.	**Mismatch between the senders' or recipients' priorities and timescales**
3.	**Others' slow response time**
4.	**Poor grammar and layout**
5.	**Too many internal (employee to employee) emails**
6.	**Unclear subject line**
7.	**Too many attachments**
8.	**Overuse of CC'd**
9.	**Overuse of Reply to All**
10.	**Out of Office messages that are out of date**
11.	**Poor housekeeping (users taking up valuable storage space on the main server)**
12.	**Over-flowery signatures and backgrounds (take time to download)**
13.	**Too much reliance on email at the expense of other mediums**

Figure 54

How can you use email even more effectively to leverage 'edge' or margin?

____

____

____

What other additional ideas for the effective use of email could you introduce to your business?

____

____

____

What other tools, methods or practices can you adopt that will enable you to get more from email?

____

____

____

For help use:

- ❑ the F1 key.
- ❑ the Help icon on the main tool bar.
- ❑ for Microsoft products – the Office Assistant.

For further information:

http://office.microsoft.com/en-gb/training

Chapter 9

Managing Energy and Overcoming Distractions

- Managing your energy
- Case Study 16
- Energy Tracker
- Plan your day
- Maximise your energy/time mix
- Utilising gaps in the day
- Gap-filler List Pro-forma
- Acknowledge the rhythm of the week
- Case Study 17
- Work from home
- Travel time
- Dealing with distractions
- Handling paper
- Case Study 18
- Filing paper

Managing your energy

An alternative way of getting more from time is to notice that there are occasions where one unit of 'time currency' seems to have more purchasing power than it does on other occasions.

This is connected to energy levels, which affect our ability to focus on tasks. Managing energy and planning time accordingly can offer a fantastic return on investment.

Many people will already recognise that their energy is affected by the time of day and might even refer to themselves as being 'morning' or 'evening' people. Some people also find that their energy fluctuates through the course of a working week, a month or even a year. This will of course be influenced by many things – what we eat and what we drink, how much sleep we have and how much exercise we take, can all impact upon our ability to cope with the rigours of day-to-day life.

It may even be that some people we work with, and some tasks that we do, energise us. They give us 'ZAP' – whilst others seem to drain our reserves and slow us down – in other words, they 'SAP' us.

Being aware of natural body rhythms and identifying those things that add value and help us to be energised will enable us to plan more of these things into our schedule. At the same time, understanding what detracts from our ability to deliver and editing those things out of our plans, will help us to be increasingly effective.

Case Study 16:

Using peak time

Making use of a unit of time when energy is high will enable far more to be achieved than using a similar sized unit when energy is low. Athletes make good use of this in planning their training programmes. They focus on completing a smaller number of high quality practices, rather than a high number of low quality practices and, as their bodies cannot stand the volume of practice they actually need in order to perfect their performance, they supplement this physical training schedule with visualisation exercises.

In the same way, if we can identify our peak (or prime) times, we can then plan and prioritise the day so that high energy time is utilised for complex or high-value tasks, whilst periods of low energy might be better used for simple, low-value tasks – or even as an opportunity to refuel or to re-energise.

Energy Tracker

By completing the Energy Tracker below (Figure 55), you will get a 'feel' for the peaks and troughs in your day. You will probably need to keep records for three to four days (longer if possible) before you can recognise a clear pattern.

Each column represents one hour. Use the first column to equate with the start of your day and every hour thereafter record your energy level. Zero represents you feeling 'normal'. The scale rising to +10 shows you to be increasingly energetic, whilst the scale falling to -10 represents your energy level decreasing incrementally.

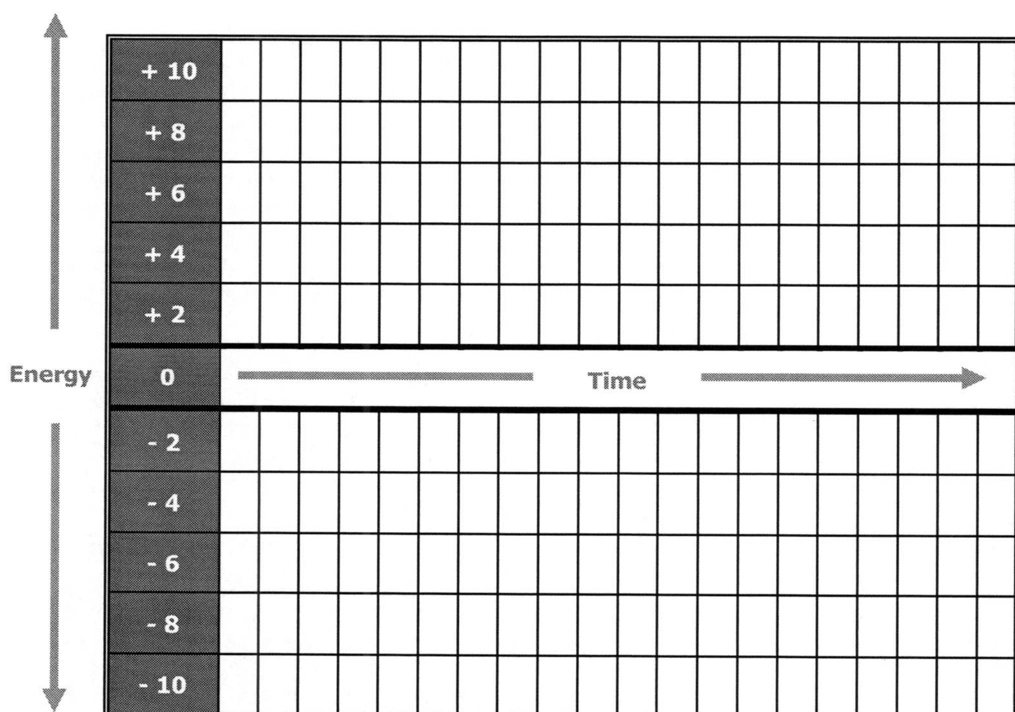

Figure 55

Plan your day

The peaks that you record are measures of the extent of your high energy and represent time that should be highly valued and used for dealing with tasks that demand drive and focus, whilst the troughs represent periods of low energy – and possibly low motivation – where drive, focus and concentration might all be hard to find.

What tasks or interactions should you plan to complete during your peaks?

____

____

____

What tasks or interactions should you plan to complete during your troughs?

____

____

____

Once you have some good data you can set it beside the Daily Task Tracker (Figure 22), and draw some conclusions as to what impact your energy is having on your ability to achieve. This may prompt you to think about planning your day differently.

Maximise your energy/time mix

- ❑ **Book time with yourself** – you may for example decide to protect your high energy time by blocking it out in your schedule. This would also be a good time to put your phone onto divert or over to voicemail, just as you would if you were attending a meeting with other people.
- ❑ **Deal with 'drop-in' visitors** – find a way to protect yourself from drop-in visitors – tell people that you would rather not be disturbed. If necessary change location and find a quiet place to work.

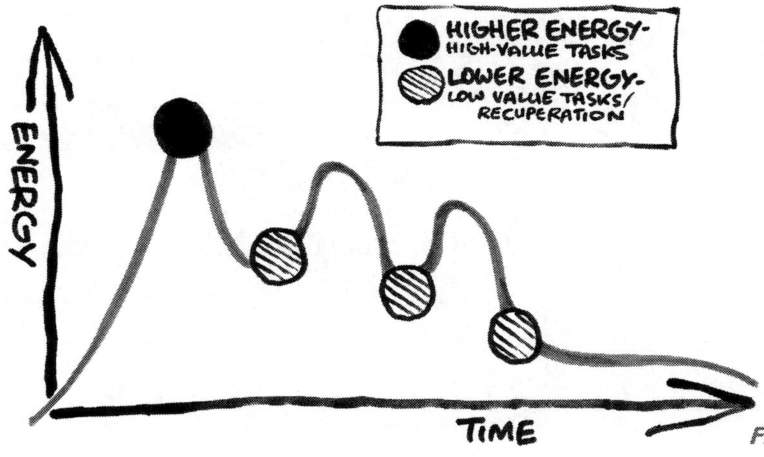

Figure 56

- ❑ **Try "Yes, and..."** – with a little thought, you can guide colleagues away from your high energy time and channel interruptions. If someone asks can we have a 'quick chat?', use the "Yes and ..." response. "Yes, and I'll be finished with this in about twenty minutes." "Yes, and shall we combine it with some lunch? Shall we say one o'clock?"

Set some conditions to saying "Yes". Your visitor has turned up at your desk because it is a good time for them to have a meeting – that does not mean it is necessarily a good time for you! Do not reward inappropriate behaviour and allow other people to plan your time – take control!

- ❑ **Manage your emails** – be disciplined with yourself. Allocate time in your troughs for dealing with the bulk of your emails, saving the difficult and complex for when your energy is high.

Utilising gaps in the day

Most people will realise that they do not have large chunks of uninterrupted time to use at their discretion. Once travel, meetings, projects and tasks have been planned into the day, the remaining time can be quickly taken up by unplanned interruptions, phone calls and emails.

Increasingly, if the day is being filled with important things, there will be a need to find a way to process the 'little things' – which of course are ideal fillers for gaps in the day. Find a way to store these 'little things' – which by definition are things that can be delayed – if they had to be done now, they would be part of the day's plan!

The key to this is to store gap-fillers straight away, in other words do not be tempted to use scraps of paper, yellow stickies or the margins of newspapers!

Gap-filler List Pro-forma

The example below shows three different sorts of gap-filler jobs which can be stored on this sheet. (For a blank version of this pro-forma, see Appendix 6.)

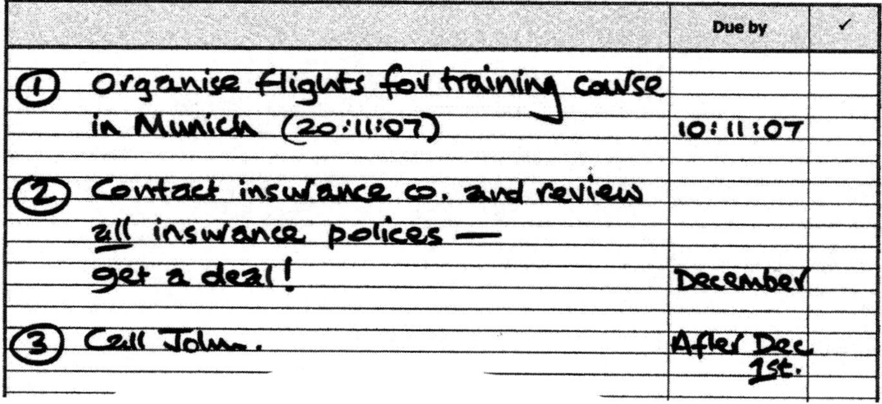

	Due by	✓
(1) Organise flights for training course in Munich (20:11:07)	10:11:07	
(2) Contact insurance co. and review all insurance polices — get a deal!	December	
(3) Call John.	After Dec 1st.	

Figure 57

For each gap-filler, identify a date by which it needs to be done and then simply review the deadline column on a daily basis and pick out any things that need to be completed in the short term.

In the meantime, whenever you have a few spare minutes, when you are low in energy or in the lull between one commitment ending and the next beginning, you will always have a ready list of things to do, which on the one hand will help you to utilise your time fully and on the other will prevent these 'little things' taking over large chunks of time, that could be used for other more important things.

- ❑ **Take breaks** – be honest with yourself. If your energy is low and you are not able to get things done, take a break, have a drink, take a walk or even have a power-nap. After any of these you are likely to be revitalised and able to be much more productive.

- ❑ **'Chat to' lists** – encourage people to save the things that they want to discuss with you on a 'chat to' list, for one hit at a time that suits you and your energy best. You could also gather things that you want to tell them onto a similar list, in exactly the same way.

This will greatly enhance the quality of your meetings, as both parties will find that some things that they wrote down during the day (which in the old days they would dealt with immediately by walking to your desk, sending an email or picking up the phone) no longer seem quite so important. By having a 'chat to' list you have got rid of this interrupter in the short term and realised that with some tasks, if you can delay them long enough they actually tusrn into something that can be dumped!

Set aside a time in the week with your key reports to go through your 'chat to' lists. They will quickly get the habit and will save things up for a later discussion, *if* they can be assured that they will have some of your time.

- ❑ **Schedule your meetings** – when you are invited to a meeting and you are given an option as to when it will take place, think about what part you will need to play and decide on its relative value to you before you agree a time.

Acknowledge the rhythm of the week

Once you have good records of your energy level over a day, they will give you a ready guide to your 'rhythm' through the week and you can plan accordingly.

If you are an early morning or early week person and you will be expected to deliver an impactful presentation, then it would be more appropriate to offer a time when you are high in energy – early in the day or early in the week. If the meeting is low value and is likely to overrun, choose a time late in the day, late in the week and perhaps also have your reasons prepared as to why you need to leave on time!

Case Study 17:

Living in the right time zone

Sports people have learnt not to fight their natural body rhythms. Competing in different time zones has meant that British boxers for example have failed to perform at their best because it felt as though they were fighting in the middle of the night – had they been at home, they would have been!

For this reason, one British football team, before travelling to Eastern Europe to play an important game, began to live on 'Eastern European time' several days before they actually travelled.

In general, it will take one day to fully acclimatise to each hour of time difference – something that should be kept in mind by the business traveller, if they want to perform at their best!

Work from home

If you have any discretionary choice in planning your week, try to work from home on Fridays – and finish the working day on time! What a great way to begin the weekend!

Think about what you can do to set the tone that will help everyone to get the best from the next few days. Clear your work things away and do something proactive to start the weekend positively.

Use Friday for administration, dealing with your email backlog, and proactively planning the next few weeks. Use the impending weekend as a spur to activity – as most people use the last day before going on holiday. Get on top of your job, clear your desk and take a full weekend to recuperate. (For more ideas on working from home see Chapter 10).

Travel time

If you have to travel, try to do it on a Monday and not on a Sunday. A Sunday flight will inevitably mean that you begin to think about travelling from lunchtime on Sunday – this not only puts a dent in your weekend, but impacts on the weekend experience of those you love and live with as well.

Dealing with distractions

Having identified your high energy time, it would be a pity to lose the advantage gained to distractions or interruptions. Use the list below to help you select the things that distract and frustrate you, diverting you from the things that you plan to do – there may be others that are relevant to you, but which are not listed here. Add them to the list.

• Telephones • Poor meetings • Personal disorganisation • Poor delegation • Lack of focus • Too much routine work • Company culture • Poor communications • Indecision and delay • Inability to say "No" • Too much paper • Lack of priorities • Too much reading	• Unclear responsibilities • Inability to complete tasks • Lack of personal discipline • Unwillingness to change • Too many tools or processes • Poor systems • Email • "Could you just..." jobs • Crisis management • Drop-in visitors • Open plan offices • Involved in too much • Travel

What are the things most likely to prevent you from using your time effectively?

____

____

____

Be aware that each of these potential barriers to success will fit into one of three groupings (see The Three Boxes, page 18): focus on addressing things within your control (Box 1, things that you can **Change**) and things you can **Influence** (Box 2) and do not waste your energy battling against things that you can do **Nothing** about (Box 3).

If everything seems to be in the third group, you may want to have a conversation with your boss, or think about finding a job that is more suitable to your skill set.

Time-waster problem-solving process:

Find a colleague and invite them to brainstorm some solutions to work-related issues with you. You might introduce this as an activity during a team meeting – encouraging colleagues to work with each other to problem solve real issues that are relevant to them – and probably to the wider team as well.

In pairs, take the role of **Partner 1** and **Partner 2**.

Partner 1 begins by introducing their first choice barrier to success:
"My problem is..."

Partner 2 responds with a million-and-one ideas:
"Why don't you...?"
"Could you try...?"
"Have you thought of...?"

After which, **Partner 1** has the opportunity to reply:
"Well, from the above, I cannot..."

... and once the list has been cleansed of illegal, immoral or completely outlandish suggestions, there should be some ideas which both partners can work on to establish an action plan for positive change.

Then **Partner 1** and **Partner 2** switch roles and repeat the process.

Time-Waster
Actions (**Partner 1**):

____

____

____

Time Waster
Actions (**Partner 2**):

____

____

____

Addressing these will not only make you more effective, they will help you to manage your stress levels as well!

Handling paper

One of the biggest time wasters and potential distracters is paper and...

'...if in doubt, throw it out'

For each piece of paper, ask:

- ❑ Do I need to print it off?
- ❑ Does this exist in a different format?
- ❑ Will I ever need to access it again?
- ❑ Would it really matter if I had not got it?
- ❑ Who else will have copies?
- ❑ Do I need all of it, or just some of it?

Case Study 18:

The 31 piles system

During the Second World War, General Montgomery was in charge of the British Eighth Army in North Africa. At one stage he made his headquarters in a converted railway carriage, which had a long boardroom style table. As he received communications, he actioned the things that he needed to do and the remainder of the tasks he left in a pile on his desk – one pile per day.

By the end of the month, he had 31 piles and no desk space! So he simply placed a waste bin at the end of the table beside the first pile and moved everything along one space. His theory being that if any of the things that he was unsure about had turned out to be urgent or important, either he would have noticed or someone else would have told him and at that stage it would have been actioned!

In his own way, Montgomery was working with the 4 D's, applying a 31-day delay (just in case) to the things that he decided to dump.

Many people like to keep things on their desk ('in sight, in mind'), which may well go against companies' clear desk policies. Cut down the amount of paper you receive at source.

Do not ask for people to send information or if you do, ask for it electronically and as an executive summary.

There are some real benefits to having a clear desk – for a start, it says something positive about you. Having a tidy workstation will give out signals to your colleagues and any visitors about your capabilities and personal organisation, in the same way as how you dress, how you talk and whether your car is clean does.

Filing paper

Having a clear desk will help with concentration, enable you to work faster and make it more likely that you will remember what you do for longer. All of which means you will feel less pressure, will be more creative and will be likely to improve your problem-solving skills.

As you receive paper, apply the 4 D's – dump as much as possible and then use a desk file or trays to organise the rest, as shown below:

Do it! Delegate it! – but manage the person. Have a plan for the day – plan in some time to actually do this work.

Delay it! – but set a deadline by when you will do it.

Separate the 'dead from the living', the day-to-day from long term.

When? Schedule a time! Edit (i.e. trim down any printed material before you store it to read). Do you need the whole magazine or just part of one article?

Store and circulate.

In addition, organise less immediate work in line with your core areas of activity, using similar headings to the files held in Word and Outlook (see Chapter 5). Use a drawer for each core area of activity, using sub-files to hold data about the component parts. So, for a core activity headed 'Staff', sub-files will be individuals' HR files, holiday or training records, or perhaps delegated tasks – exactly as they would be if you imagine your hierarchical files in Word.

File papers regularly and also weed out the files periodically, otherwise they will become too large. Establish geographic zones reflecting the importance or frequency of use for specific documents:

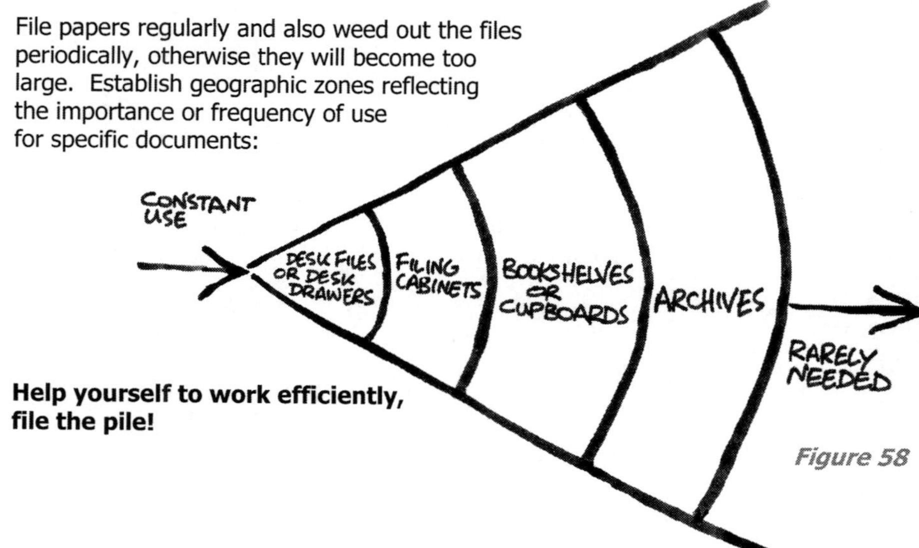

Figure 58

Help yourself to work efficiently, file the pile!

Chapter 10

Working from Home

- Working from home
- Benefits and drawbacks
- Top tips
- Case Study 19
- Case Study 20
- Checklist of things to consider

Working from home

The last few years have seen many changes in the rhythm of working life. The common use of mobile phones, laptops, the Internet and PDAs have all enabled individuals and businesses to operate in a radically different way. Employers who once found it merely 'acceptable' for senior managers to work from home, now positively encourage other colleagues to operate away from the office, having a dramatic impact on those individuals' way of life.

On the employees' side, many have experienced a fantastic sense of freedom and self-determination. On the employers' side, this shift has allowed businesses to make substantial savings in overheads (in terms of expensive office space, and all the ancillaries that go with it), and, by blurring the parameters of the working day, has surreptitiously made homeworking staff available for work 24 hours a day, 7 days a week, 365 days a year!

Clearly, the time has come for people to think about how they will operate under this new regime and to lay down some good rules and ideas for best practice. Coping with working away from the office will demand the development of a personal strategy.

Benefits and drawbacks

What are the benefits of your working from home for you?

___

___

___

What are the benefits of your working from home for your employer?

___

___

___

What are the benefits of your working from home for your customer(s)?

___

___

___

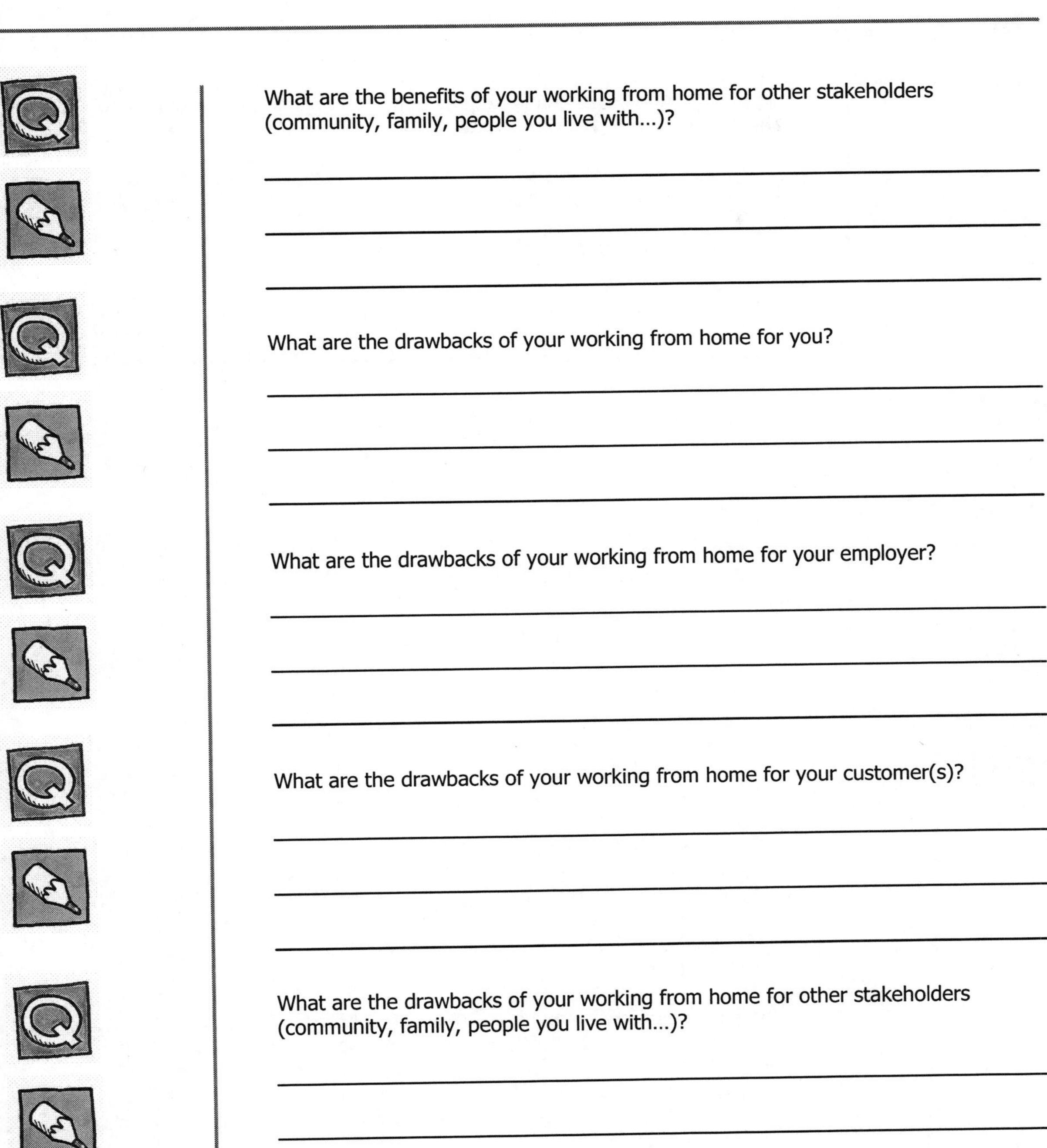

What are the benefits of your working from home for other stakeholders (community, family, people you live with...)?

What are the drawbacks of your working from home for you?

What are the drawbacks of your working from home for your employer?

What are the drawbacks of your working from home for your customer(s)?

What are the drawbacks of your working from home for other stakeholders (community, family, people you live with...)?

How well you handle working from home will be influenced by a number of factors. The first may be your attitude towards work in general.

Imagine a continuum – at one end stand the people who **work first and play later** and at the other end, stand people who prefer to **play first and work later**.

Mark where you would position yourself on the line.

Work first **Play first**

How do you believe this will affect your approach to working at home?

___

___

___

What strategies could you adopt to help with this?

___

___

___

Every office environment contains individuals, each with their own preferred working style, who, if they were honest, would position themselves at different points on the line. Over time, office norms will have been established to cater for the differences in their working preferences – these norms will be affected by the type of business, the prevailing management style, and the layout of the office, as well as the personalities involved.

Whatever the office environment, there may be some who have the time to chat by the coffee machine and then to network around the office before settling down to functional tasks. Often these social animals need to have imposed deadlines, i.e. a meeting that starts at a fixed time, or a report or project that needs to be completed, before they can discipline themselves to actually sit down and get on with the functional parts of the job that they need to do.

At the same time, and in the same office, there will be other people who turn on their PC as soon as they arrive at work, set their own targets and get straight on with tasks and projects – keeping interaction with colleagues to a minimum. These people may need to be encouraged to get out of their chair and network a little more!

It is inevitable that these two groups will have a very different approach to working from home. The former might find themselves feeling increasingly isolated and lacking in motivation, whilst the latter will use the lack of interaction with colleagues as an opportunity to withdraw further into themselves.

This means there can be no one formula for success in working from home, but below are some ideas which may help.

Top tips

- ❑ **Establish a routine** – decide at the outset what the parameters for your working day will be.

How much time do you intend to allocate to your job? What else should you (or would you like to) build into your day? Will the working day run 9-5, or would it suit you to work in chunks? What are the total number of hours you intend to work?

It is important to find answers for all of these questions, otherwise it is possible that for some people the working day (and hence personal productivity) will shrink, whilst for others the working day will have no defined end and will overspill into their private lives.

- ❑ **Deal with interruptions.** What is an interruption to you? Do you see drop-in visitors, the telephone or emails as being interruptions? Are they stressors to you, or do you welcome them?

Who or what do you see as interruptions? What will be your strategies for dealing with them?

- ❑ **Manage your environment** – where will you physically do your work?

If you have an office or study at home, decide how it can best be set up so that you can work in it most efficiently. Do you have a comfortable chair, a good desk, the equipment and materials that you need? Is the environment set up to allow you to do the sort of work that you need to do? Can you leave your work on your desk, or will you need to consider security and privacy?

How will you set up your office space? What will you need to make it user friendly?

____

____

____

If you do not have an office or study, where will you work – in the kitchen, in the dining room, on the settee...? Are these places conducive to you doing a good job and getting the most from your time?

Wherever you have to work, it is important to set things up in a way that enables you to be as efficient as possible. If you are sharing a space with other people, you need to be able to close down and clear away – so having good files and storage systems will also be important.

Case Study 19:

How it was

Alex works from home and has tried to turn it to his advantage. He feels good that he no longer has to spend 5 hours on his round trip to the company head office and believes that he is more productive working from home. However, he misses the interaction (at all levels) with his colleagues and finds that the line between work and private life is becoming increasingly blurred.

For the first few months of working at home, Alex enjoyed being able to start his working day later than he would when he had to travel. He found space at the kitchen table (once his partner and kids had left for the day) and used his laptop and mobile phone for the bulk of his work. Increasingly, he felt the need to answer all phone calls and e-mails immediately, because he was afraid that his colleagues might think he was not at work if they could not actually see him or hear his voice. His briefcase and some plastic bags became his 'hi-tech' filing system.

Alex managed to get through a reasonable volume of work during the middle part of the day, although he found it difficult to work once the family arrived home, which led to increased pressure on him and conflict with his partner, as he would return to work once the kids had gone to bed. Things came to a head one morning when Alex found himself unshaven, in his pyjamas and doing his e-mails whilst making breakfast for his son, who was on school holidays...

Case Study 20:

How it is now

Alex realised he needed to raise his game and that if 'working from home' actually means 'not working in the office' then there were in fact a number of other places that he could work. Sometimes he still goes to his company head office, because it suits him to and he also makes use of office space in his company's regional offices, or in client's offices.

He has decided to use technology to make his life as easy as possible and has reorganised the way that he has structured his PC, his database and e-mail, so that information can be stored and found more easily. He has cut the amount of paperwork he generates and carries to a minimum, by having better paper filing systems (which he actually uses). He avoids the temptation to print off information that can be kept in electronic form and he throws away as much received paperwork as he possibly can.

When he works from home, Alex has found a space that he can call his own, where he can leave his PC switched on, and he has established ground rules with his family around computer access and security and privacy.

Alex has changed his working methods and has realised that to have a successful day, he needs to have planned it the night before. So, as part of his close-down procedure, he reviews the day he has had and, in outline terms, plans the next day. This means that he establishes the time that he intends to start and finish work in advance. He ensures he is prepared for any meetings and decides from his lists of tasks and projects how he is going to allocate the rest of his working day. He also leaves some space for e-mails, interruptions and crisis.

If he is not visiting head office or clients, Alex usually goes to his home work space at about 07.30 and clears his inbox. He allows 30 minutes for this, after which he shaves, showers and has some breakfast.

By 08.30 he is ready to walk his children to school, with the dog. He has discovered a whole new social life at the school gate and with other dog owners, who think he is somebody who has got his quality of life sorted out, being able to do these sorts of things on a working day.

Alex feels good that he already has a chunk of work behind him and that he has had time for 'the things that matter' with his family. His boss and his colleagues have proof that he is 'at his desk' and he is able to return, energised, to do some more focused work from 09.00, when experience tells him the work phone will start to ring.

He has changed his phone message so that it now says: "Thank you for calling Alex X. I am either in a meeting or on the phone at the moment. Please leave your name, number and a BRIEF MESSAGE and I will get back to you."

Rarely during the day does he take calls as they come in, preferring to work for a concerted period of time and then to respond to calls when it suits him. (Like all of us, he can look at the caller ID and he may decide that some calls need to be taken immediately!)

Alex rewards himself with a break mid-morning when he also takes a chunk of time to look at mails and respond to his calls. He stops for lunch, which he never used to do, but again finds this means he returns to work refreshed.

If he is working from home in the afternoon, he will do a chunk of work followed by phone calls and e-mails before walking to the school to collect his kids. If he feels like it, he spends some time playing with the kids and usually finds time afterwards to do a couple more hours before closing down for the night.

This closing down process involves reviewing the day and finalising his plans for the next day, so that he can take off his 'working head', put on his 'home head' and get on with life.

Chapter 10 – Working from Home

Checklist of things to consider

- ❑ **What is the physical space that you will work in like?** – Does a good space exist, or will you need to create a new space somewhere?
- ❑ **Can you make use of other office spaces?** – Build site visits into your plan, especially if you thrive on face-to-face interaction.
- ❑ **What equipment will you use?** – Would you rather use a dedicated landline than a mobile phone – if you use a mobile phone, would it be worth getting a headset? Have you got broadband, if not can you get it?
- ❑ **What impact will your working from home have on the people that you live with?** – Do you need to contract with them? What ground rules will you need to lay down? How can you encourage people to give you space and quiet? How can you model best practice?
- ❑ **Should you clear away?** – Do you need to tidy up at the end of each working session – either for privacy or out of respect to other people who are sharing your space?
- ❑ **How will you store your work?** – With information already stored on your PC, how much paper-based data do you need close to hand? Consider having levels of data. The more current it is, the closer geographically it should be to hand. Records and historical data can be filed out of sight and out of reach. Find a place to keep an in-tray for post, pending and project work.
- ❑ **How will you manage your interaction with other people?** – How will you deal with interruptions? How will you cope with loneliness and boredom? Do you enjoy being interrupted, or is it a chore? Identify your interrupters and develop a strategy to deal with each. Encourage people to save up interruptions for when you want to be interrupted.
- ❑ **How will you manage visitors?** – Is your home office the best place to bring customers or clients for a meeting? Will it support the image that you or your business need to create? Consider site visits or using other hosted meeting places – but do not be tempted always to go to their office, as this will have a major impact on your time utilisation and has a high opportunity cost.
- ❑ **Find ways to reward yourself** – What would a reward look like to you? Taking breaks, stopping for a drink or fresh air will actually help you to re-energise – a walk, a trip to the deli, beginning to prepare an evening meal could be a refreshing distraction, which will also set you for success in the evening.
- ❑ **Measure and enjoy your success** – Think of those occasions when you have had 'a great day'. What have you done? How can you build more of these kinds of things into your schedule?

- ❑ **Create some variety** – Do not allow yourself to be bogged down in the mundane. Plan to do difficult, high value tasks when you are at your best and use the success of achieving these to energise yourself.
- ❑ **Dress for success** – Consider how you dress when you work from home. Would it help you to feel like you are actually 'going to work' if you were dressed for business? What message would this give out to family, friends and neighbours, who might otherwise think your working from home equates with being semi-retired, making you fair game for 'could you just...' jobs.

Think through your strategy for working away from the office – make it work for you and ensure that you get some of the benefits that flexibility can bring!

Appendices

- **Appendix 1 – Goal Recording Pro-forma – Chapter 3**
- **Appendix 2 – Daily Task Tracker Pro-forma – Chapter 4**
- **Appendix 3 – Action Planning Pro-forma – Chapter 4**
- **Appendix 4 – Tasks Delegated To Pro-forma – Chapter 6**
- **Appendix 5 – Meetings Pro-forma – Chapter 7**
- **Appendix 6 – Gap-filler List Pro-forma – Chapter 9**

Appendix 1 – Goal Recording Pro-forma

Dream Goal:							
Performance Goals		Process Goals (First Steps)		Process Goals (Next Steps)		Detail	✓

Appendix 2 – Daily Task Tracker Pro-forma

Daily task tracker **Name:** ______________________________

Date: ______________________________

1	2	3	4	5	6
1A-3C	**Box I-IV**	**Start Time**	**Task**	**Time Taken**	**Ideas for Smartening up Time & Task Management**

You are welcome to reproduce this sample pro-forma. Alternatively copies can be downloaded from http://www.stepsystem.co.uk/stepsystem-downloads.html

Appendix 3 – Action Planning Pro-forma

Project or Task Title

Who	What	When

You are welcome to reproduce this sample pro-forma. Alternatively copies can be downloaded from http://www.stepsystem.co.uk/stepsystem-downloads.html

Appendix 4 – Tasks Delegated To Pro-forma

Tasks delegated to:

Who	Action Required	Priority	Date of Meeting	Due by	✓

You are welcome to reproduce this sample pro-forma. Alternatively copies can be downloaded from http://www.stepsystem.co.uk/stepsystem-downloads.html

Appendix 5 – Meetings Pro-forma

Meeting:		Notes	Action Plan		
Date:	People:		Who?	What?	When?
Time:					
Place:					
Agenda:					

Appendix 6 – Gap-filler List Pro-forma

Gap-filler List:

	Due by	✓

You are welcome to reproduce this sample pro-forma. Alternatively copies can be downloaded from http://www.stepsystem.co.uk/stepsystem-downloads.html

Booklist

John Adair	***'Effective Time Management'***	Pan 1988
Polly Bird	***'Teach Yourself Time Management'***	Teach Yourself Books, Hodder & Stoughton 1998
David Brake	***''Dealing With E-Mail'***	Dorling Kindersley 2003
Christina Cavanagh	***'Managing Your E-Mail'***	John Wiley & Sons 2003
Stephen R Covey	***'The 7 Habits of Highly Effective People'***	Simon & Schuster 1990
Herbert Fensterheim & Jean Baer	***'Don't Say 'Yes' When You Want To Say 'No'***	Futura Publications 1991
Nancy Flynn & Randolph Kahn	***'E-Mail Rules'***	Amacom 2003
Tim Hindle	***'Manage Your Time'***	Dorling Kindersley 1998
Max Landsberg	***'The Tao of Motivation'***	Profile Books Ltd 2003
Sally McGhee	***'Take Back Your Life! Using Microsoft Outlook To Get Organized and Stay Organized'***	Microsoft Press 2005
Monica Seeley & Gerard Hargreaves	***'Managing in the Email Office'***	Butterworth – Heinemann 2003
Declan Treacy	***'Clear Your Desk'***	Random Century Business 1991

Index